MANY BLACK WOMEN OF THIS FORTRESS

KWASI KONADU

Many Black Women of this Fortress

Graça, Mónica and Adwoa,
Three Enslaved Women of
Portugal's African Empire

HURST & COMPANY, LONDON

First published in the United Kingdom in 2022 by
C. Hurst & Co. (Publishers) Ltd.,
New Wing, Somerset House, Strand, London, WC2R 1LA
© Kwasi Konadu, 2022
All rights reserved.
Printed in the United Kingdom by Bell and Bain Ltd, Glasgow

Distributed in the United States, Canada and Latin America by
Oxford University Press, 198 Madison Avenue, New York, NY 10016,
United States of America.

The right of Kwasi Konadu to be identified as the author of
this publication is asserted by him in accordance with the
Copyright, Designs and Patents Act, 1988.

A Cataloguing-in-Publication data record for this book
is available from the British Library.

ISBN: 9781787386976

This book is printed using paper from registered sustainable
and managed sources.

www.hurstpublishers.com

CONTENTS

It was my choice. It was my life and I didn't have to live it like that. But that was what life offered me in the way of being a woman and I took it. I grabbed hold of it with both hands.

Rose Maxson, in August Wilson's *Fences*

1. Map of West Africa and the Mina Coast, featuring São Jorge da Mina, c. 1560. (ANTT, Colecção Cartográfica, no. 166, Livro de Marinharia, de João de Lisboa, 1560).

2. Portuguese map of West Africa, c. 1563. "Mina" refers to the region and to São Jorge da Mina. ("Nautical Chart of Portuguese Cartographer Lázaro Luís, 1563," archived at the Academia das Ciências de Lisboa. Photograph by Joaquim Alves Gaspar, March 2008).

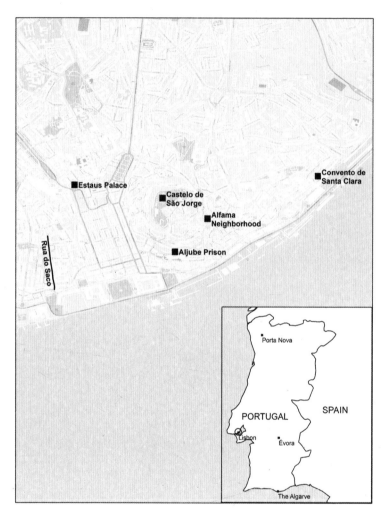

3. Lisbon and the places mentioned in the book. (Commissioned by author).

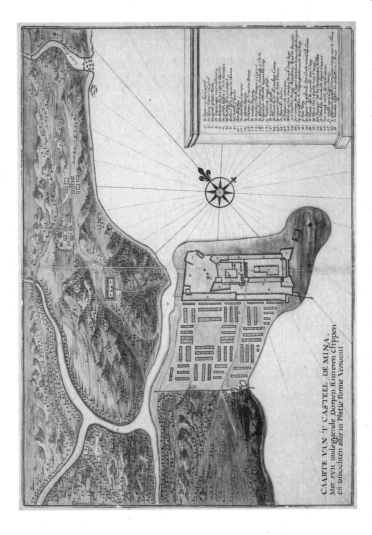

4. Map of São Jorge da Mina, the Benya River, and nearby settlements, c. 1665. (Wikimedia Commons).

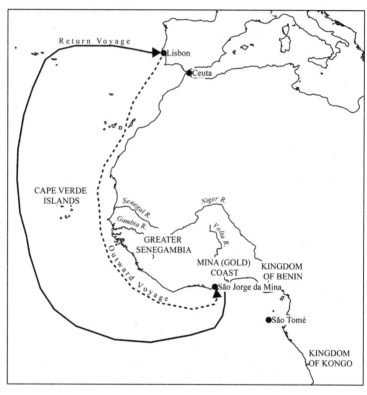

5. Sea route between Portugal and the Mina (Gold) Coast.

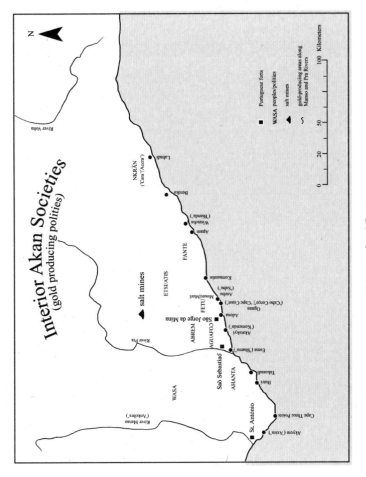

6. Mina (Gold) Coast.

INTRODUCTION

We will therefore not write about that which is unknown to us.

—Duarte P. Pereira, navigator and fortress captain

Ɔhɔhoɔ ani akɛsekɛseɛ, nanso ɔmfa nhu hwee.

Though the stranger's eyes may be big, s/he does not use them to see anything.

WITH CLERICS OF THE Inquisition passing judgment, Portugal's king watching the condemned from his seat on high, and the global city of Lisbon buzzing with foreigners, this elderly African woman's presence in the Portuguese capital might have represented the defiance of empire, if only slightly obscured by that of other human cargo, naked and soaked with humidity and half-sobs. Her and their presence was more the parading of captive souls, condemned to the travails of the Inquisition. She had already been baptized, in name and by the voyage that exiled her from African lands of gold, a fate shared by captives pillaged from other African territories, who together accounted for a sixth of Lisbon's total population. Convicted and dumped into a murky medieval jail cell, Graça, the elegant one, awaited trial for crimes against the faith, embodied in the Catholic Church, the nerve center of Portugal's empire. Meanwhile, the captive Africans whom Graça passed en route to the ecclesiastical prison awaited the enslaving rites she had experienced decades earlier: at the altar of sale and baptism, their subservience and subhumanity yielded to the "empire of God." As one theologian reasoned, god "chose Portugal for his own empire."[1] Sitting in her dungeon cell, with her male inquisitors occupying the top floor of the Gothic building, Graça was the "king's slave" in status. But in her own skin and in her lived experiences, she belonged to a people and a place far from Lisbon, to polities and villagers that endorsed her beliefs and that made a seventy-year-old enslaved woman a threat to a global maritime empire.

As Graça examined her circumstances, she felt the villagers and kinfolk in Africa constituted her homeland, as water makes

3

the sea. The home-grown way of life and coded wisdom of her people must have made all the truncated experiences of imprisonment, exile, and condemnation a little more bearable, knowing as she did that perhaps other defiant African women like Mónica and Adwoa might wash up on the shores of Lisbon to face the Inquisition—the empire's immune system. And there was so much truth there; their whole homeland, called the Mina (Gold) Coast, seemed somehow to be intransigent in the face of Portugal's forces of religion and firepower. What the men of empire did not know, or their pretensions prevented them from seeing, was that Graça, Mónica, and Adwoa wielded certain powers of their own. And their powers, their personal advocacy and boldness in the face of sexual violence, religious dogma, and the authority of men of empire, were far from invisible in the world of the fifteenth and sixteenth centuries.

⌘

Documentary evidence for the lives of African women and girls is exceedingly rare for the sixteenth century and even scarcer for the fifteenth century. Almost all African women and girls whom Portuguese mariners encountered in those years were rendered nameless in their accounts. Men from Portugal were the first early-modern Europeans to arrive on the West African coast, and their global empire, built with African gold and bodies, left a large but incomplete paper trail. An earthquake in 1755 destroyed most of the royal archives and of Lisbon, obliterating what we could potentially know. Newly discovered records for Graça's homeland, however, offer exceptions to the paucity of documented lives. Graça was born between 1470 and 1480, though she entered the strangers' chronicles decades later. In the 1490s, the Mina (Gold) Coast featured African female merchants like Briolanja, among other women mentioned by name or in passing or inscribed as enslaved persons. The same records reveal that Portuguese women were also merchants but working in tandem with male slave traders. Isabel Machada and Beatriz Esteves were paid to care for captives procured by male merchants, usually on the basis of shared costs, but these women also purchased captives under their care. Carer and slaveholder Marta Fernandes paid "for a very young little slave who was given to her to be treated at shared cost." Most white women residing at the main Portuguese fortress on the Mina (Gold) Coast, then called São Jorge da Mina (now Elmina Castle), were exiled and not necessarily unmarried, and a few fortress captains did bring their wives with them. White women were usually few in number compared with the large roster of enslaved African girls and women, like Graça and Mónica, divided as they were among male residents and officials of the fortress. Some of these bonded women and girls hailed from greater West Africa, while others were Africans or women of African descent from Portugal. In the mid-sixteenth century, two manumitted women of African descent came from Lisbon and worked in the fortress's oven-house and infirmary. These women held estates worth up to 60,000 *réis*, but since the manumitted and enslaved did the same menial work in Lisbon and throughout the empire, they were rare anomalies in sharp contrast to the widely shared experiences of women like Graça, Mónica, and Adwoa.[2]

There are very few studies or life stories of African women before the nineteenth century, and recent scholarship on African women starting in the late seventeenth century remains focused on how they made use of their relations with European (and mixed-race) men and the opportunities offered by them. In other words, those men constituted an integral axis around which these women gained status, accrued property, experienced mobility, wielded nominal authority, or succumbed to sexual and other acts of violence.[3] It is also widely assumed that African women and women of African descent in Atlantic Africa even in the

fifteenth and sixteenth centuries owned property, wielded influence, and exercised some power on account of their reliance on
European (and mixed-race) men. Surely this is an important
aspect of complex intercultural and intercontinental relations,
though relatively few African women occupied those indetermi-
nate or intermediary roles. This book, *Many Black Women of this
Fortress*, takes a different view, arguing that there were more
often ordinary African women and girls who did not submit to
empire and their male European agents. Instead, they stood up
for themselves and exercised spiritual and female powers independent of European and African men in an age of maritime,
slaving, and missionary empires.

In the formative era of European global empires, pioneered by
Portugal, we know the least about the number of enslaved and
freed African women subjected to both Portuguese commerce and
religion, and even less about their lived experiences, especially in
large parts of the African mainland where miscegenation was rare.
Though the Portuguese monarchy's prohibition of unions
between Portuguese men and African women had mixed results,
it would seem that for the women of Graça's, Mónica's, and
Adwoa's world in Atlantic Africa, miscegenation was uncommon
apart from on the islands of São Tomé and Cape Verde.[4] Their
experiences run counter to popular notions. And those lived experiences came face to face with a global empire and its terror-
inducing institutions such as the Inquisition. The intertwined
lives of African women like Graça and Mónica who served in the
premier colonial outpost of the Portuguese empire in West Africa
provide another narrative for stories of freedom and nonviolent
Atlantic exchanges; indeed, their insurgent spiritual ideas and
actions defy the all-too-common plotline of movement from slavery to freedom. Graça and Mónica relied far less on their connections with the "Atlantic world" for their status and power, instead
activating their own forms of "female power."[5] While the archival

sources are rare, the experiences of these women cohere with those of dozens of other women in the same period and same places, making them windows into a collective history.

Among the young and old, enslaved and manumitted, unconvinced and baptized African women and girls of the fifteenth and sixteenth centuries were many who defied the global empire. While some liaised with European men along the African coast, these ordinary yet bold women pushed back against new forms of captivity, racial capitalism, religious orthodoxy, and sexual violence, as if they were self-governing. Looking at those formative features of modernity through the lives of these women, we can see the world fashioned by empires as a space at war over beliefs, precious metals, commodified bodies, and goods. Our guides to this evolving world are three African women—Graça the elderly captive, Mónica the manumitted spiritualist, and Adwoa the eyewitness to the failure of religious conversion and Portuguese colonization.[6] *Many Black Women of this Fortress* reveals the insurgent ideas and actions of these women, which is to say the exaltation of their cultural norms and forms, as well as their spiritual bearings, nurtured on local African soil. Theirs is a narrative, or set of stories, written from obscurity, from the forgotten and overlooked records of empire. By drawing attention to these lives, we dare to approximate the complexities of what happened, offering close-ups of modernity's gestation. These women invite us to consider anew the world shaped by global empire and racialized capitalism in the crucial fifteenth and sixteenth centuries.[7]

✠

Portugal's march to global empire began with the capture of the North African caravan terminus and seaport of Ceuta in 1415. Buoyed by African gold, the Portuguese erected fortified trading posts along the coasts of Africa, Brazil, and Asia—the São Jorge da Mina fortress on the Mina (Gold) Coast was the most important in Africa. By the 1540s, when the exiled Graça stood in front of the Inquisition, she witnessed Portugal's capital of Lisbon exporting theology, textiles, metals, and foodstuffs, while importing from Africa gold, ivory, captive peoples, dyestuffs, and textiles. From India and greater Asia, the Portuguese acquired varieties of cotton cloth and silks, resin, diamonds and other precious stones, musk oil, hardwood, spices, carpets, and furniture. Situated on the longest river in the Iberian Peninsula, Lisbon became the empire's leading seaport and the largest city in Iberia with a population of fifty to seventy thousand by the mid-sixteenth century, when Mónica, too, found herself exiled to Lisbon. Lisbon also became the center of the empire, residence of the royal family, and home to the first members of the Society of Jesus (the Jesuits). Portugal's Inquisition and the Jesuits were operative in the early 1540s as a Catholic response to the rise of Protestantism in Europe, and they established themselves across a global network forged by empire. While the Jesuits functioned as agents of empire and colonization along the oceanic and land routes of trade, gaining missionary success and accruing political and economic power in the overseas colonies, so did the Inquisition at home in Portugal and through its tribunals abroad.[8]

Nascent and still in flux, the Inquisition extended religious authority throughout Portugal and its imperial network, sponsored by close cooperation between the monarchy and clergy. The synergy between royal and religious leaders helped define identity for the nation and empire, drawing a sharp distinction between Old Christians (*Cristão-velho*) of pure blood, race, and religion and New Christians (*Cristão-novo*) and a cast of cultural and religious others. While the Jesuits were establishing roots in Portugal, the Portuguese were losing commercial ground on the Mina (Gold) Coast, failing to develop a sustainable Christian community and, even more so, to hold on to the few believers residing in and around São Jorge da Mina. All Portuguese overseas possessions remained under the authority of the Inquisition, and so the foreigners viewed the Mina (Gold) Coast through the optics of São Jorge da Mina—a political and spiritual extension of Portugal. "Power was at the heart of the Inquisition," the historian Toby Green reminds us, "and thus, inevitably, did religion enter the province of politics." Unlike medieval and papal inquisitions, Spain and Portugal's Inquisition came under the monarchy's direct control and spread its influence to their colonies, with fear percolating every layer of society. Portugal's ruling elite applied its jurisdictional authority abroad as it did in the homeland, though there were no tribunals in Africa. Consequently, Africans like Graça and Mónica were brought to stand trial in front of the Lisbon tribunal, the principal court adjudicating most inquisitional cases.[9]

Readers unfamiliar with the Inquisition, an institution entangled with Graça and Mónica's story, should bear in mind that Portugal adopted from Spain a three-tier structure for its tribunals. Led by an Inquisitor General, with the assistance of three deputies, the General Council remained the highest agency, setting policy and supervising local tribunals. Two to three inquisitors, aided by three to four assessors, headed each local tribunal. At the second tier, external experts evaluated suspicious writings and priests confessed prisoners, while also accompanying inquisitors in both secret and public trials and delivering sermons before a victim's sentence. Public prosecutors, lawyers for the accused, clerks of the court, and minor officials made up the rest of this second tier. Finally, commissioners appointed by the Inquisitor General covered the nation as a whole, especially districts without tribunals, and collected testimony about suspects. Unpaid informers assisted these commissioners. A suspect's inquisitional process followed a routine: arrest and detention under scrutiny, interrogation and torture, a bill of indictment, a defense, and an elaboration of judgment reached by a majority vote. Proceedings were secret and prisoners were often unaware of the exact charges or the evidence against them; they were provided with a lawyer but to extract a confession. This lawyer was assigned by the Holy Office, and he was accountable first to it and then to the defendant. The lawyer remained absent from interrogations and had no access to the transcripts of the victim's testimony. Prisoner and lawyer were sworn to secrecy as were other members of the inquisitional process. Property confiscation and public humiliation in penitential dress usually preceded sentencing, which could involve imprisonment, further religious instruction, or execution. Neither Graça nor Mónica was executed, but their fates, like the shape of their stories and the challenge of writing them, were significantly different.[10]

The lives of Graça, Mónica, and Adwoa intersected with foreign institutions like the Catholic Church, the Inquisition, or the judicial apparatus of the Portuguese empire, producing the documentary evidence for their existence. However cleverly retrieved, their stories remain as inviting as they are slanted and limiting, contorting what we can and cannot know about their intimate, private lives. Portugal styled itself as *the* empire of god, as it sought out the global currency of gold from these women's homeland. There, and elsewhere, the strangers weaponized belief, deploying baptisms and conversion to break down the private, interior space of personhood. For they realized something crucial to invading a people's consciousness and belief: that through baptism or conversion, the invaded psyche might turn against itself, serving the stranger's dogma and eviscerating its own ideas, down to the molecular level. If achieved, intrusions such as these were more lasting in their effects than any military aid, political sway, or trade goods. After all, Portugal's was a missionary and maritime empire, embroidering theology and trade, setting the patterns of engagement, and laying the architecture for subsequent Europeans seeking empire and gold, then captives and other commodities. The idea of the world in Europe was theological and moral in the sixteenth century, before shifting into a secular, geographic, and economic idea in the next century. Tethered to this shift were multifarious forms of violence. Violence involved racialized slavery and religious ideologies that brought inquisitional terror upon the world, for Christian theology had long shaped cultures of violence in Europe and in its global offshoots. The lives of Graça, Mónica, and Adwoa reveal how theology and slaving played the role of midwife in the violent birth of a modern and modernizing world. Such violence also bled into the imperial archives, determining what life stories can be recovered from them.[11]

Writers and scholars know just how difficult it is to research and narrate the stories of women. Like a passenger looking out an airplane's window from take-off to piercing the skies, the further we move away from a moment—the past—the more daunting it is to sense what was on the ground, why human action took shape in certain ways and not others. Recognizing these challenges is important, and even theorizing about them has its place. Some scholarship has tried to reconstruct the lives of women through theory in the absence of evidence, even insisting on theorizing or fictionalizing African women's lives, instead of wide-angled, deep digging and anguishing over fragmented details. Scholars and writers interested in such lives need not turn to fiction and claim it as history nor use theory to instantiate history and take the place of evidence. Too many lives are unrecoverable, and we must accept that. To claim records or archives as inherently problematic is no more useful than saying the ocean is made of water. Even diaries and memoirs are constructed, built-up versions that often stray from straightforward truth-telling. Writers can no more claim the sources used to tell stories are problematic, when this is a given, than position themselves as saving, rescuing, or liberating women from whatever judgment or classification scheme froze them in time, in a record.[12]

Records are our means of transportation to that foreign land called the past. Though we can visit, we cannot inhabit it or experience the world as our subjects did. And there is no transcending act with which to leapfrog over this impossibility. What is essential, then, is to know our subjects' world as closely and as deeply as possible, so that the settings and the ways women like Graça, Mónica, and Adwoa moved through them feel real and human. We know records flatten much of this three-dimensional look and feel of human lives, but that is what records are designed to do, and therefore writers need to focus less on what is missing than on what is found in the archives. Evidence in whatever archive is always partial and often random. As Kiera Lindsey writes, "All archives are inherently idiosyncratic." Encountering archival gaps does not require a rush to fill them with inventive tales, precisely because gaps are invitations to focus on overlaps, where creative license gives way to careful, methodical examination to reveal recurring clues that inform the (re-)construction of human lives. Crafting life stories into a narrative means drawing on historical context as the content of informed speculation, but it also means getting away from the idea of documents as sources or the most important data points. Archives holding documents are not brokers of what we can and cannot know, because there are gaps in our knowledge that no amount of research will fill.[13]

Many Black Women of this Fortress is about the intertwined yet wide-angled lives of three fifteenth-to-sixteenth-century women who served in the premier colonial outpost of the first global empire in West Africa. The modern world took decisive shape in these centuries of maritime empires, global slaving, and the formation of racial and religious ideologies that intrude on the present. These themes are brought into new and sharp relief when viewed through these women's experiences. Graça was an elderly woman when she was brought in front of the Portuguese Inquisition in 1540, from West Africa to Lisbon, to stand trial for crimes against the Catholic faith. African relations to land and labor were rooted in kin relations to the earth and the immaterial. Any rupture of the bonds with ancestral land and with kin in the flesh and in spirit was crucial for marking a person as enslaved and as a believer. Graça was enslaved, laboring as the property of the Portuguese monarch, but her material and affective bonds remained with the local villagers and her spiritual bonds with her deceased parents, whom she ritually fed and communed with regularly. Born around when the first Portuguese sailors arrived on her shores in 1471, she became the first African, if not the first woman, to appear before the newly established Inquisition. When viewed up close, the events surrounding her life, and that of the two other women—Mónica Fernandes and Adwoa—instructively reveal a more complex story, filled with ongoing violence, attempts to heal, and denial of victory to a maritime and missionary empire.

While Graça was enslaved for over three decades, baking bread and caring for Portuguese men in the infirmary, she struck the empire at the core of its self-identity, because the strangers believed themselves to be a people of pure blood, race, and religion. She was also entangled in a love triangle, in which participants used the Inquisition, which safeguarded the empire's self-identity, to eventually exile her from her homeland to a Lisbon monastery, where she would spend the rest of her life imprisoned. Mónica was also exiled, first within the Portuguese forts on the Mina (Gold) Coast, and then to Lisbon to face the Inquisition, as Graça had. Graça and Mónica would have known each other. Though Mónica was manumitted, she performed the same work as the enslaved women in the fortress. She, too, rejected Portuguese claims to purity, and so, rather than yield to Catholicization, she chose African medicines and therapeutic rituals in the face of ridicule from other "black women" and sexual violence from Portuguese men. And that violence persisted with the full knowledge of enslaved "black men" who also served or were in contact with Portuguese men of the fortress. Though Maria was baptized, she was also known as Adwoa, a Monday-born Akan female. The imperial control which the Portuguese envisioned over their subjects was thwarted, precisely because the empire hinged on controlling trade relations and this required partners to accept Catholic tenets—as evident in baptism, in naming, in dress, in language, and in the rituals of the faith. To reject these was to challenge empire and the male structures of power that made slavery, race, and religion work in favor of empires. Even more remarkable is that these challenges came from the enslaved, manumitted, and gendered—those least likely to make history and often erased from male-dominated productions of history.[14]

Graça, Mónica, and Adwoa were not women on the margins of history, though at times they were marginalized. Their paths intersected at the São Jorge da Mina fortress, itself connected to the wider world through the Portuguese empire. Along with the fortress at Arguin, off the coast of northwest Africa, São Jorge da Mina was the foremost edifice and symbol of the European presence in Atlantic Africa, serving as a working model for imperial expansion in Africa, Asia, and the Americas. Portugal's transition from Catholic nation to Christian empire occurred when contact with and exposure to Atlantic African cultures intensified. Indigenous spirituality and foreign religious ideology thus became a central arena in which relations or conflicts between Atlantic Africa and Christian Europe were worked out. Graça's coerced travels to Christian Europe, to stand trial in Portugal, took place in 1540. In the six decades leading up to her trial, gold from her homeland doubled Portugal's public revenue, and it remained significant in the next three decades, providing purchasing power for Asian commerce and maritime expeditions, collateral for loans, and luxuries for the elite. Graça's exile from her homeland came at the hands of the resident vicar in the fortress, who declared her a nonconformist and rebel against the empire's theology and authority. Though Graça was branded the "king's slave," the vicar's determination only hinted at the real issue: Graça had struck the king and the empire at the heart of its proclaimed self-image of purity. Especially vexing was that the blow came from an African, a woman, and a slave who was scripted to serve rather than undermine that self-representation. Though Graça and Mónica's denunciations were contrived, the target—a set of spiritual ideas and technologies found among "the black people"—was both real and revealing in these women's world.[15]

The big idea that animates this book is how ordinary women in times of extraordinary global change lived, worked, and believed within the web of empire, yet against its seminal instruments of commerce, religious dogma, and slaving and racial ideologies. The violent and often non-consensual coalescence of these instruments formed our modern world. The stories of Graça, Mónica, and Adwoa give us a unique snapshot of global empire and its ideologies and institutions, the most notorious of which is the Inquisition. These women and their supporting cast provide a close-up examination, like no other, at the level of human relations central to life in the early-modern world and to the workings of empire. Through their optics, we can view empire as missionary and colonial, pushing the chronology of (attempted) European colonialism to the fifteenth and sixteenth centuries, but foregrounding the early pan-European scramble for African commodities, captives, and converts. If one believes that Europeans simply tapped into existing systems of "African slavery," these women's stories turn that idea on its head, for Portugal ran a slaving enterprise on African soil, importing all the legal, institutional, and monetary structures necessary for transatlantic slaving. The women's lives offer the clearest evidence for the shortcomings of the slavery-to-freedom plotline and of the peaceful exchanges lauded in Atlantic histories.[16] The Atlantic world was peripheral to them and most Africans in the fifteenth and sixteenth centuries, and their insurgent ideas and actions defy what we have assumed or come to know about African women and girls confronting a global empire and all its machinations.

THE CAST MEMBERS

Adwoa — Villager in Adena; also known by her baptismal name Maria.

Manuel de Albuquerque — Captain and governor of the fortress-city of São Jorge da Mina, c.1536–40.

Margarida de Albuquerque — Manumitted woman of African ancestry; one of Mónica's friends.

Gonçalo Toscano de Almeida — Vicar (the bishop's representative) of the São Jorge da Mina church (c.1546–48).

Jerónimo de Azambuja — Friar and inquisitor in Mónica's case.

Beatriz — Enslaved woman of African ancestry belonging to João III (c.1521–57).

Catarina — Enslaved woman of African ancestry, named Madu, belonging to João III.

Clara — Manumitted woman of African ancestry who once belonged to João III.

Lourenço Correia	Factor (trader) at São Antonio fort (c.1540–42); served as Mónica's godparent.
Lucrécia Correia	Manumitted woman of African ancestry whom the bailiff Bento Roiz had brought from Portugal to São Jorge da Mina.
Maria Domingues	Arrived at São Jorge da Mina in 1542 and served there.
Dr. Álvaro Esteves	Member of the king's High Court of Justice, and inquisitor and prosecutor for the Lisbon tribunal. Esteves was responsible for the king's legal proceedings; he also served as rector of the University of Coimbra, a center of learning for the elite.
António Feio de Castelhaco	Jailor of the inquisitional prison in Lisbon; married to Caterina da Fonseca.
Ana Fernandes	A woman of African ancestry who came to São Jorge da Mina from Portugal.
Marta Fernandes	Manumitted woman of African ancestry who worked in São Jorge da Mina.
Mesia Fernandes	Manumitted woman of African ancestry, working in the oven-house at São Jorge da Mina.
Mónica Fernandes	Born close to São Jorge da Mina, enslaved, baptized, and then manumitted.

THE CAST MEMBERS

Francisca	Manumitted woman of African ancestry who served the bailiff Bento Roiz; she was a companion of Mónica.
João Gonçalves	Servitor of Manuel de Albuquerque; he testified in Graça's case.
Graça	Elderly and enslaved African woman about sixty or seventy years old at the time of her inquisitional trial; she was born between 1470 and 1480.
Bárbara Lopes	A woman of African ancestry who hailed from Portugal and worked in the oven-house at São Jorge da Mina with Graça.
Pedro Lopes	Vicar of the São Jorge da Mina church, which, from 1534, fell under the authority of the bishop of São Tomé.
Manuel Manriques	Prosecutor on the Lisbon tribunal in Graça's case.
João da Mata	Margarida's lover and Graça's supervisor in the communal oven-house. Regarded as a master baker, he arrived at São Jorge da Mina after 1536.
João de Melo	Former bishop of the Algarve and, later, archbishop of Évora, he presided over Graça's case and delivered the final judgment.

Rui de Melo — Captain and governor of São Jorge da Mina, c.1552–56.

Diogo Pacheco — Vicar of the São Jorge da Mina church during Mónica's time.

João Vaz de Paiva — Unmarried officer and physician at São Jorge da Mina during Graça's time.

João Rodrigues Pessanha — Captain and governor of São Jorge da Mina, c.1583–86, and alleged sexual predator who faced the Inquisition in 1588.

Margarida Rodrigues — A "black woman," though described as "mulatta," she hailed from Portugal and was a lover of João da Mata.

Estêvão Soares — Former factor at São Jorge da Mina, whom Mónica once served.

Diego Ortiz de Vilhegas — Castilian priest and theologian who served Portuguese monarchs on matters related to astronomy and navigation; tutor of João III; and bishop of São Tomé (under which São Jorge da Mina fell) from 1533 until 1540, when he assumed the bishopric of Ceuta.

1

"A RENEGADE FROM THE CATHOLIC FAITH"

Obi mmua n'ano nni ɔ.

One should not remain silent to the point of being pronounced guilty.

I

THE CASE REACHED NEAR finality, then the ruling came.
The year was 1540, and it too was ending. On the upper floors
of the Aljube prison, men of authority—inquisitors, bishops,
lawyers—convened a hearing of the Santo Ofício da Inquisição
(Holy Office of the Inquisition) to decide the fate of an African
woman, imprisoned in a cell beneath them. She hailed from
Africa's Mina (Gold) Coast, then a key source of Portugal's gold
and key site of its triangular slave trade in the Gulf of Guinea.
The gulf between her fate and their verdict closed sharply.
"The Deputies of the Holy Inquisition and the Ordinary rule
that," the head inquisitor announced, "having examined these
records, namely, the prosecutor's charges and the evidence
given, it is shown that the defendant, Graça, being a Christian,
said certain sticks of hers were her god, in addition to the other
facts referred in the records. And yet, considering the quality
of the evidence, as well as the fact that the defendant, after
being made a Christian, was not instructed or indoctrinated in
our Holy Faith, we sentence the defendant to life imprisonment, where she will be instructed in the Faith. We assign her
as her prison the Monastery of Santa Clara of this city of
Lisbon, and we charge in conscience the Mother Abbess and
nuns of the monastery with taking very great care in her
instruction and salvation."[1]

To those men, Graça was a disposable captive facing justice for
her crime—nonconformity to Catholic dogma—and their
empire's conception of belief and fairness had triumphed. She

was, after all, a "slave" of the king of Portugal. And Portugal now had a global empire. King João III stood as the ultimate slaver because all captives not in private hands belonged to him. João III was also a fanatical believer. If belief was the engine of the empire and slavery was premium fuel, the king was the sole driver and the passengers were key institutions propping up the monarch's rule. The Inquisition became the foremost institution of the empire, the vehicle at whose helm was the king. When João III came to power in 1521, he inherited not only the rudiments of a far-flung empire from Manuel I, but also Manuel's acquiesce in Spanish policy when he married Isabella, heiress to Spain's united crown. In their marriage contract, Manuel agreed to persecute heretics and expel non-Catholics, feeding Spain's Inquisition and its desire to rid the kingdom of these undesirables. Jews and Muslims had to be baptized or face expulsion; those who stayed had a grace period of thirty years, ending in 1534. Manuel also hoped his male offspring would inherit a crown uniting Spain and Portugal. No male child came of Manuel's marriages to three Spanish queens, but Spain's inquisitional pressure and a new cast of religious councilors in João III's court pushed the king toward creating Portugal's own Inquisition in 1536 and recruiting many Jesuits from Italy (though most were Spaniards). Fanatical about his Inquisition, João III ardently supported the Jesuits, calling them apostles, and even telling a fellow noble he would give up part of his empire to have the entire Society of Jesus in Portugal, as imperial servants. The first Jesuits reached Lisbon in June 1540, where they were confined to serving the royal court, which they described as "more like a religious house than a court." Graça arrived around September, entering that religious house and the throes of the religious and racial tensions animating the global empire.[2]

Graça was an ordinary person living in an age of empire and of extraordinary yet uneven engagement with the wider world. Her Africa did not seek out Europe. Rather, western Europe followed

Portugal's plunge into western Africa, hunting for gold and then for lands from which captured and captive peoples would forcibly depart. Serial acts of abduction and enslavement, then incarceration and exile, such as Graça intimately experienced, birthed our modern world. That world's most crucial fault line was belief—a signal clash among cultures, understood by imperial Portugal as irreconcilable religions. The world for Portugal and its empire was one of orthodoxy, or right belief and conformity to Christian doctrine, on one hand, and heresy, or erroneous belief and nonconformity to Christian dogma, on the other. Founding myths authorized the rightness and fitness of Portuguese orthodoxy: from the time of the first king, Afonso I, the kingdom and its rulers believed themselves providentially chosen to convert all people by conquest and evangelization; as they possessed their god's favor, his intervention on their behalf was assured. Religion became the most important marker of human (racial) difference, and so baptizing then convicting Graça was essential for the preservation of empire and enslavement across it, because her pre-baptismal beliefs (linked to her race) stood in the way of Portugal's ordained destiny. In turn, differing beliefs were attributed to racial and religious deficiency or superiority, for only Portugal had god on its side. Portugal's turn to conquest placed cultures outside Christendom, and even new converts viewed with suspicion, under inquisitional terror. From what is recoverable in documents emanating from the Inquisition, Graça bore witness to the terror of empire and the modern conjunctions of slaving, race, and belief. If it is possible to recover her story, the tensions in her world of hegemony and condemnation, we must put empire and those intersections on trial as well.[3]

II

Graça was born between 1470 and 1480, either before or after the first Portuguese mariners reached her homeland in 1471 but certainly before the São Jorge da Mina fortress was built in 1482–83. Erected on a peninsula near the village of Adena, this military and trading base—the most vital fortress in Atlantic Africa—was built under the direction of Diogo de Azambuja, its inaugural captain. And yet this did not happen without conflict with Adena villagers. The uneasy truce between Adena and the São Jorge da Mina fortress formed the setting for Graça's everyday life, one saturated with violence. There is no slavery without violence and terror. Graça may have been one of the enslaved females assisting the three women from Portugal who remained with Azambuja, serving the sixty male residents of the fortress and working in the infirmary and the oven-house. Even so, she spent most of her time with the villagers of Adena, speaking their language and not Portuguese, and relishing the amnesty offered by these interactions from the physical, sexual, and spiritual violence endured in the fortress. How Graça became a "slave" of João III and what might have been her prior everyday life is unknowable, but her captivity, her new name, and her daily life working in the oven-house of the fortress began when she was somewhere between the ages of nineteen and twenty-nine. Capture or purchase brought her into the world of captivity, to labor for and serve her captors, and baptism sealed her fate as a chattel of João III and his god.

Graça was baptized in the church of São Jorge da Mina, properly called the church of Nossa Senhora da Conceicão (Our Lady of the Conception). When asked, "Who was the priest that had baptized you, and what was his name?" she said, "I do not know his name." Africans like Graça were unfamiliar with the perennial Christian–Muslim antagonisms, the near-uninterrupted wars between them. Baptism worked as a substitute for conquest, by extending that war to Africans as impure moral and racial enemies to be evangelized and reduced to the status of (baptized) non-human. Baptism also worked as a substitute for slavery as a state of war—a race war—by registering peoples of Graça's kind as black heathen objects of Christian conquest. Baptism for Graça and non-European peoples was not a singular event, confined to one meaning. Changing one's name, reneging on pre-baptismal cultural forms and ideas, and professing the faith all went with baptism. These requirements, however, applied to every African, including elites who partnered with the Portuguese in respect of arms, trade, or protection. They too were made subordinate to the Portuguese king, the pope, and the god of the empire.

Though Graça's Christian identification flowed from her baptism, baptism was for most enslaved peoples a meaningless ritual conducted in a mysterious language or, worse, a form of European witchcraft and a sign of their cannibalism. Catholicism for those under Portuguese or Spanish captivity was an alien ritual that slavers had little interest in diffusing among their chattels. In 1534, the head of New Spain (modern Mexico) wrote, "The enslaved blacks at the sugar mills and associated facilities are not given the time to attend church services, they do not know the basic prayers, and the majority do not even understand Spanish." Though conversion was envisaged as the primary reason for enslavement, in order to save souls, primal greed for precious goods and metals took precedence. The worst offenders who were targeted were thus those who kept something of their indigenous beliefs and cultural forms after baptism. At the height of trading in gold and captives on the Mina (Gold) Coast, the king of Portugal incentivized conversion: two *justos* (gold coins worth 380 *réis*) went to each Catholic priest for every boy from Adena, "up to a total of fifteen a year, whom they trained as choirboys." The captain of the fortress would also receive two *justos* for each boy, and one *justo* for each adult converted to Christianity. Maintaining the empire and its dependency on gold, goods, and commodified humans triggered this strategy, and yet it failed. Most villagers, even those with frequent Portuguese contact, preferred their "heathen names," and consulted ritual specialists and healers in the village. Graça's constant exchanges with these Adena villagers illustrate how anemic the spell was that Christianity cast over their lives.[4]

When asked, "Who had been your christening godparents?" Graça replied, "João Machado and Graça de Leão, who, after they completed their time at Mina, had returned to Portugal." We know as much about Graça de Leão, after whom Graça was named, as we do about most women who labored in the fortress, including the three undocumented women present there from its founding. Graça de Leão was one of seven exiled women sent from Portugal to the premier fortress in the empire, while João Álvares Machado was resident at São Jorge da Mina in the 1490s. By the time of his departure in 1499, when Graça was in her twenties, Machado had surrendered his food allowance to Captain Lopo Soares de Albergaria together with gold earned from selling an enslaved woman allotted to him, to local people who traded at the fortress. These enslaved women were principally imported from the Bight of Benin, through the Portuguese island colony of São Tomé, and were often exchanged for Mina gold and then exported to Portugal and Spain. Some remained to labor in the fortress alongside Graça, while others were sold to local merchants and suppliers of gold. Paid just over one mark and six ounces of gold for two years' work, Machado took only the ounces with him when he left, having spent the rest. Residents like Machado had multiple stints at the fortress, and so that may not have been the first or the last of him. João Nunes, the supervisor of the oven-house where Graça worked, also had multiple spells of duty.[5]

Though baptized, Graça knew little about the rudiments of Catholic orthodoxy, and this would remain so. Neither the priest who baptized her nor her godparents taught her how to cross herself (*signum crucis*) or how to recite the Our Father (Pater Noster) and Hail Mary (Ave Maria). At best, Graça was only able to mumble the first words of these prayers in Latin. Most Africans subjected to inquisitional terror came before the tribunal because of their alleged ignorance of the faith. But they were not the only ones utterly incapable of responding to questions of faith put before them. Besides Muslims and Jews, Portuguese peasants and working-class people fared only slightly better than Africans in their knowledge of Catholicism, the majority receiving no more than a salt-and-prayer baptism in Portugal or overseas outposts like Mina. Even while Graça offered food to her direct ancestors and communed with them at night, in her shared quarters near the oven-house, folk superstition and medicine, including talismans and "spells," was deeply embedded among people in Portugal well into the nineteenth century. These folk beliefs proliferated in part because illiteracy was so high in mid-sixteenth-century Europe—at over eighty per cent—but it was more pronounced for women and so they were unduly targeted as purveyors of erroneous beliefs.[6]

And so, when asked, "Do you know the Creed?" Graça could not utter a word of it but said, "The priest Pedro Lopes is now beginning to teach it to me. I had been baptized in the time of King Dom Manuel, and no one had ever taught me the Pater Noster and in Latin nor the Ave Maria nor the Creed." Manuel I ruled Portugal from 1495 to 1521. The overlap with João Machado's tenure at Mina places Graça's baptism between Manuel's accession to the throne in 1495 and Machado's return to Portugal in 1499. And yet it is strange that a nineteen- or twenty-year-old would be baptized at that age if she had been born, as her records stipulate, in the São Jorge da Mina fortress. Graça was, by her captor's reckoning, between sixty and seventy years old when imprisoned in Lisbon, which makes her older than the fortress. The fortress, then, must have signified in the records the surrounding settlements. The closest was Adena, which was under the political overlordship of the Eguafoɔ, though it was sometimes contested by the polity of Fetu. The Eguafoɔ and the citizens of Fetu and Adena formed the spatial arc of Graça's community, and perhaps her homeland, while her strongest bonds derived from her visiting and being visited by Adena villagers.

The Eguafoɔ and its subordinate village of Akatakyi never converted to Catholicism though they traded with the Portuguese. In contrast, Fetu's ruler was baptized in 1503 and yet endured a contentious relationship with the foreigners. The cohort of baptized peoples in Fetu dissipated, and further conversions failed as the chapel of Santiago erected in the capital square deteriorated. Fetu's ruler then joined forces with a "black Christian" merchant named João Serrão to oust the Portuguese from the entire Mina (Gold) Coast. If Graça was born in Mina, she originated from Fetu, Adena, or Akatakyi, or from among the Eguafoɔ, and was enslaved as a young adult. Captives of local origin could be sold, and local rulers might exchange them with officials at São Jorge da Mina. In 1529, the ruler of Akatakyi or the Eguafoɔ supplied five captives as "gifts" to the Mina captain Lopo Soares de Albergaria.[7] Since São Jorge da Mina remained under a royal monopoly, and Adena became a Portuguese protectorate after achieving independence from Fetu and the Eguafoɔ with Portuguese support, Graça was the king's property. The king of Portugal claimed that half the villagers in Adena were "Christians and have received the water of baptism," urging, "they must be defended, protected, and instructed ... [because] they are our vassals." By the time Graça was enslaved, and then baptized, her ideas about culture and belief were formed, and this might explain her life under Portuguese captivity for several decades and also help us understand from which faction of Adena she derived spiritual succor.[8]

As the king's chattel, Graça's status shifted while at the same time remaining fixed. These subtleties presaged features of the broader transoceanic slaving regimes from the time of her inquisition onward, when captive Africans would be valued as currency, commodity, and producers of capital and opulence, managed by European empires. Though their statuses might have altered slightly—captive, slave, manumitted—their existence as *negro* (black) and as *gentio* (unbeliever) remained remarkably stable, even fixed. The life of the black–slave–heathen in European and overseas slave societies was an uninterrupted inquisition.[9] Seeded in her baptismal name was an early transatlantic form of being dispossessed of personhood while simultaneously being the possession of another. In the idiom of the sixteenth century, those enslaved in the Iberian Peninsula were recorded as, and often called, *peças* or "pieces," a unit of value. When Graça became the king's slave, her servile status was confirmed by the denial of a second or family name, certifying kinlessness and an existence as the property of another. Graça was her baptismal name, but tucked away in the African language she spoke was a non-slave name, used when in the company of "black people" from Adena. Portuguese officials at São Jorge da Mina hoped the ritual of Mass and roll call would help baptized or captive Africans "hear their Christian names repeated, because ... all the other [converts] after leaving the company of Christians and returning to their village, call themselves by heathen names." Out of the four women working in the oven-house, two, namely Graça and Beatriz, did not have second or family names. Not surprisingly, both belonged to the king of Portugal. The other two women in the oven-house at the time of Graça's trial were Margarida Rodrigues and Bárbara Lopes, who hailed from Portugal, having been born or baptized *and* emancipated there before being exiled to Mina. Emancipated they might have been, but Margarida and Bárbara had as much control over their lives and their fates as Beatriz and Graça did.[10] All were slaves of various indiscernible degrees.

The status among indigenes who interacted with São Jorge da Mina after baptism made a difference in the kind of name they received, including Graça. The ruler of Fetu, Sakyi, was renamed Dom João after the king of Portugal, and a son of the Great Akan's ruler was baptized António de Brito, after a former Mina captain who served there and died in 1545–46.[11] But if Graça was baptized, as she claimed, then she should have had a Portuguese first and second name. There is nothing in the records to explain this, and yet the naming pattern which Graça bore applied to the bulk of Africans reduced to transatlantic chattels. Graca's and Beatriz's enslaved status, racialization and kinlessness were signified by their dispossession of a family name. And this shared sense of dispossession would make Beatriz less of an enemy to Graça, while the common experiences of Margarida and Bárbara may have cast them as principal informants or denouncers of her.

III

Living near the fortress's oven-house, Graça "was a kneader in the said oven house, baking bread for the people." Bread was the staple of the Portuguese diet. The oven-house supervisor received a monthly supply of flour, and employed women of the fortress to make bread. Regulations dictated that four salaried and four unpaid women, aided by some enslaved females, kneaded and baked the bread. Room and board replaced salaries for unpaid workers. Graça's salaried female co-workers received the lowest annual wage (12,000 réis) compared with the male workers (whose numbers shifted between fifty-six and sixty-three) stationed at the fortress in the sixteenth and seventeenth centuries. Twenty to thirty enslaved women and men served the needs of the fortress at all times: construction and repair or loading and unloading a ship's cargo fell to at least ten male captives, who also doubled as porters and laborers, while at least six female captives cooked, washed, and cleaned for the Portuguese residents. Graça and the women of the oven-house also toiled as nurses in the infirmary, and were routinely subjected to the everyday sexual violence coded in the records as "other duties pertaining to them."[12] Enslaved girls and women, who were not counted as members of the fortress, remained at the disposal of residents. By 1519, there were eighteen enslaved African women serving in the houses of high-ranking officials and residents. Graça, then between thirty-nine and forty-nine, was the mother of four sons while working in the oven-house. The production of "mulattos" was a sign of the Portuguese male presence across the globe, and at least fourteen children issued from these eighteen women—six daughters, eight sons. Graça had the most children of any one woman, and her sons, like the children of all enslaved women, inherited their mother's chattel status.[13] We cannot prove that rape resulted in these children, but neither can we be certain of consent.[14]

Each day, the women working in the oven-house provided every resident with four loaves of coarse baked bread. Women, too, received rations of bread, along with oil and vinegar. Breads were made from imported wheat or locally procured millet or maize. "The Negroes of the Castle Damina," a Dutch observer wrote, "bake very fine Maize bread, which looks like Wheat bread. They make it with incisions, like Leiden Rolls, and also manage to bake them so hard that they can remain good and hard for three to four months." To produce maize bread, male captives in the fortress would repair the ovens with a mixture of clay, straw, and sand, while Graça and the other women prepared the dough with cereal grains pounded and mixed with water. The fire set in the oven needed time to reach desired temperatures and then be cleared of ash. The oven doors were closed once the dough shaped into round loaves of bread for fortress occupants and biscuits for slave ships was placed inside. Bread produced in Graça's oven fed crew and captives aboard Portuguese slave ships traveling to São Tomé, the Bight of Benin, Angola, and onto Portugal, helping satiate a global appetite for African bodies.[15]

As in late-medieval Europe, bread was eaten morning, midday, and evening, with midday set aside for the most substantial meal. These loaves were complemented by a daily flask of wine and a monthly supply of one pot of olive oil, two pots of vinegar, and a pot of honey. The Portuguese at Mina were to rely solely on imported foods—grains, oils, wines, animals. Royal decree restricted Portuguese contact with the peoples of Adena and the surrounding area, but Graça's frequent travels between the fortress and Adena flouted this rule. The fortress's apothecary dispensed medicines from Portugal as well as from herbalists in Adena. Though prohibited, Portuguese men also searched villages nearby for crops, chickens, goats, and women, despite regulations that talked about protecting the virtue of women from Portuguese in the fortress. Any officer or resident who made a mistress of one of these women could lose all his salary paid in gold. Imperial prescriptions about food or faith were one thing, but what happened on the ground in local contexts was quite another, for there were African women, including the likes of Graça, "who have lived with the Portuguese in the Castle and who manage to cook something good."[16]

A bread and starchy diet exposed the Portuguese and their captives to nutritional challenges: too much starch and too little protein. Restricted from obtaining chicken and other protein sources from Adena, the foreigners waited on livestock imported periodically from São Tomé. Graça's frequent contacts with Adena villagers and her fluency in their language and landscape removed her from this nutritional obstacle. Adena was nestled in a forest-coastal ecology, having access to yams, oil palm, fruits, seeds and nuts, cowpeas, guinea fowl, fish, domestic goats, sheep, giant snails, and grass-cutters. A high mortality rate afflicted Portuguese residents, in contrast to Graça, who enjoyed old age and longevity. Though baking bread required time and simple ingredients, Graça experimented with an assortment of breads and baked goods, and not merely the gluten-filled wheat flour variety that made for the denser bread dominating the Portuguese diet. Millet and then maize were likely substitutes. As early as 1510, the ruler of Fetu was reported as having several cornfields, and Graça and women of the oven-house learned to use gluten-free millet grain when wheat flour was unavailable or in short supply. By the mid-to-late sixteenth century, maize (*Zea mays*), introduced by the Portuguese to West Africa, had been innovatively incorporated into the farming and dietary practices of African communities. Around 1535, a Portuguese pilot claimed that maize "grows all over these [Atlantic] islands and all along the African coast and is the chief food of the people." This maize was called *zaburro* but the pilot also referred to maize as millet *zaburro* (i.e., sorghum). Maize and millet do share physical traits, so much so that the Portuguese considered millet a small form of maize (*milho miúdo*).[17]

It is not always clear from contemporary sources if observers were referring to millet, maize, or their varieties. Along with cattle, local *milho* (maize) and palm wine—substitutes when wheat failed and wine was in limited supply—were "for the white people to consume." These substitutes formed bridges that Portuguese residents crossed in their acclimatization to African foodways. Graça played no small role in these transformations over several decades, precisely because she prepared what residents ate. Visitors to Graça's homeland also paid attention to what foods "the blacks eat": oranges, lemons, citrons, nuts, peppers, coconuts, sugar cane, honey, plantains, eggplant, white and red pumpkins, sweet potato, amaranths, maize, palm oil, palm wine, goats, and sheep. Imported pigs adapted well at São Jorge da Mina but perished at Akyem, while the horse and the donkey died at São Jorge da Mina and elsewhere owing to local disease and insects. "The blacks sow *milho* grande which they call [*aburɔ*] and which in Castile is called 'Indies corn'," wrote one observer, in addition to yams, "which in this land provide an excellent staple food." Graça stood at the center of the agricultural and culinary exchanges shaping her globalizing region, experimenting and innovating with new crops alongside staple and varied indigenous foods. These foods remained predominant, but the increasing use of maize for local consumption and for slaving, as well as other imported starches, was a harbinger of things to come. Soon the local diet Graça knew intimately became dominated by starches, following the Portuguese custom. This transatlantic slave diet, so called because the new crops arrived along slaving routes and often provisioned slave ships, would change little thereafter, as various European visitors all noted the widespread cultivation of maize, plantain, sweet potatoes, yams, and rice.[18] And then Graça was condemned, not for baking bread or serving residents, but for ritually feeding her deceased parents.

IV

It was one early Sunday morning. Appearing before the vicar of São Jorge da Mina, Pedro Lopes, was João Vaz de Paiva, set to testify against Graça. Paiva held a university degree but was an unmarried officer who worked as the pharmacist in the fortress. On that seventh day of April 1540, Paiva told the vicar, "I was going to the oven-house of the fortress for some vermicelli-like pasta, and I met some black women who worked in the oven-house who were shouting. These were Margarida Rodrigues and Bárbara Lopes, women who worked at the kneading-house. I asked them why they were shouting, and they told me that Graça, slave of Our Lord the King, had some things related to sorcery and idolatry, of the heathen kind, and that they told me about it to unburden their conscience, for they were Christians."

Meeting him at the customs house, the vicar informed Mina captain Manuel de Albuquerque about what the pharmacist had told him. Before assuming the captaincy, Albuquerque had distinguished himself while serving the empire in India from 1531 to 1536, under Nuno da Cunha's local administration. He was also kin to Afonso de Albuquerque, the infamous conqueror who established Portugal's dominance in the Indian Ocean region. With only months left of his term before returning to Portugal, Captain Albuquerque ordered that Graça be at once brought before him along with João da Mata, the baker in the oven-house, together with the alleged items of witchcraft. He immediately ordered "that Graça be put in the pillory and prison of the fortress. He told the Vicar to make a judicial examination of the matter to apply the law."

That same day, Vicar Lopes went up to the pillory where Graça was held. He asked her, "Are you a Christian?" Graça said, "Yes." He then asked, "What is your name?" She replied, "Graça." "And where had you been made a Christian?" She said, "In the church of this fortress." He continued, asking, "Who was the captain at the time when you were made a Christian?" Graça answered, "The captain was Diogo Lopes de Sequeira." Sequeira was the Mina captain from December 1503 until January 1505. If "made a Christian" meant baptism, then this evidence places Graça's baptism later than the earlier estimate of 1495–99. And, yet, officials such as João Álvares Machado, one of Graça's godparents, often served more than one term, sometimes uninterruptedly. Machado might very well have returned during Sequeira's time, when Graça de Leão, after whom Graça was named, was present. Graça could have also been confused about events that had happened more than thirty-five years earlier. Hoping to pin Graça down to a specific time, the vicar asked her, "What was the name of the priest who had baptized you?" She could not remember, only saying, "He was a large man, who shortly after left for Portugal. He had lodged with the factor [trader], who was called Barros." Although she was unable to name the priest, Graça's poorly grasped Portuguese points to Estêvão Barradas, who worked as factor from 1504 to 1507. Though different surnames, *Barros* and *Barradas* were phonetically close. On this matter, Graça said no more.

The vicar then examined her antagonist, João da Mata. Mata was asked the customary questions; asked whether he wished evil or good to Graça, he said, "I did not wish her either evil or good, only that she served there in the kneading-house, just like all the others, who are under my charge because I supervise the oven-house." When asked about the alleged "spells and idols," Mata said, "It is true that, almost as soon as I arrived at the fortress, Captain Manuel de Albuquerque had told me one day to beware of a black woman who was called Graça, and not to give her anything, for people said that she was a great witch."

On the day of the incident, "I heard a tumult and hastened to it," Mata continued, "and arriving at the door I saw Margarida Rodrigues coming with a soiled clay mug in her hand, and she said that they were spells belonging to Graça and that she had more of them. Having seen this, I went out of the oven-house, where Graça had a chest. I looked between this chest and another one, and I found a clay mug out of sight between the chests, which was fixed to the floor with clay. And so was the bottom of another mug that Margarida Rodrigues had taken. And when I saw this, I asked her what the purpose of those things was, and Graça remained silent. *And I slapped her several times to make her tell the truth,* and she said that one of them was for her father and the other for her mother, so they would come there and eat, which was a custom of her land, and that custom was what black people did." The arbitrary meting out of unwarranted violence, unconstrained by considerations of gender or age, was part of the condition of being a black–heathen–slave, who did not need to transgress to be the recipient of such violence. Violence saturated the life of the black–heathen–slave figure.

Furthermore, Mata added, "Margarida Rodrigues said there were other spells about which the other black women could tell me. And, then, I told the cooper to move a box belonging to Graça, and under it we found a small wooded bowl with a base, the size of an eating vessel, with four round sticks about three or four fingers long, whitened with flour or lime. I asked her what its purpose was, and she remained silent for a little while. And then I pressed her to say what it was. She replied that it was her God, and I asked her again what she was saying, and again she said that it was her God. I ordered that the bowl be taken and kept, so it could be shown if necessary when I was asked about it." Mata said no more.

Next to testify was João Vaz de Paiva, the pharmacist who had confided in the vicar and accused Graça of sorcery. After the customary questions, Paiva confirmed what he had said earlier, that "while going to the oven-house in the morning for some vermicelli-like pasta, I had met Bárbara Lopes, a black woman, and Margarida Rodrigues, a mulatto woman. Both serve in the kneading-house and came from Portugal, and they were shouting and having words with Graça. And these women of the kneading-house, as soon as they saw me, told me to look at the spells which Graça had there. They showed me two mugs made of clay and fixed on clay-like cloth rolls, and then they found one of the mugs under a bed belonging to Graça, and they showed it to me, and inside it I saw a feather and other things which I did not care to look at because they were disgusting."

Another mug was then broken along with the one Paiva saw. "And right after that," Paiva resumed, "these women of the kneading-house told me and João da Mata, who was present, to look under a chest that was there, that we would find more spells, and that they only knew what the other black women had told them." And immediately Paiva and Mata "told *the cooper, who was present, to move a chest aside, and they found a small bowl with a base, the size of an eating vessel, with four round sticks in it, around four fingers long each.* The bowl and sticks were floured with flour or lime. I did not know which. And when Graça's mugs were found, João da Mata asked her what their purpose was, and Graça *said that it was for her father and mother, who were already dead, to come there and eat and that this* was a custom of black people."

The two men then asked Graça "what those sticks were or what was it all about, and she, leaning against the chest where they had taken them from, said with *a serious face that it was her God. And then João da Mata said, 'Your god?' and Graça said 'Yes!' with great steadiness.*" Then, Paiva admitted, "I started shouting at her, rebuking her. And at that point," Pavia recalled, "the black woman who served the *meirinho* [bailiff or officer of justice] and others told me something, in their language, which I did not know. This black woman again said that *Graça's spells* could kill no one and that she had taken the said sticks and rubbed her breasts with them." At that point, Paiva left, "shouting at the other women who were there and rebuking them." He said that he knew no more.

Bárbara Lopes, whom Paiva met on his way to the oven-house, testified next. After the case details were read to her, Bárbara remarked, "While I was in the oven-house with other black women, namely Margarida Rodrigues and Beatriz, a black woman who belongs to the King, as I was going to get a small bowl which I had under the corner of my chest to take some embers in it, I saw some clay mugs under the said bowl. I asked what it was, and Beatriz told me that it was one of Graça's spells and that under the chest there were others. I then told Margarida Rodrigues. Margarida tried to take the mugs, and Graça went for her to take them back, and they broke them. Margarida had first shown one to João da Mata and then João Vaz de Paiva; there were chicken feathers in it and white powder. At that point, João da Mata came and *slapped Graça several times while asking her what it was, and she had told him that she gave it to her father and mother to eat.* And then we told João da Mata to have her chest removed, for we black women knew that under it were other spells. João da Mata ordered the cooper to remove the chest, and under it he found a small bowl with a base and four round sticks the size of about three or four fingers each, floured white with something which he did not know whether it was lime or flour. João da Mata asked Graça some questions, and likewise did the pharmacist, but I did not hear them because I was taking bread out of the oven. *I heard people say that Graça spoke with those mugs at night and prayed over them,* but if it is so or not, I do not know." Bárbara said no more.

The vicar then turned to Margarida Rodrigues, who declared, "I will say all that I know." On the morning of April 7, Margarida confirmed, she, "being in the oven-house, was told by Bárbara Lopes that Graça had spells which were between two chests, and I went there to look and found two clay mugs with chicken feathers in them and fixed on clay. I picked up one of them and showed it to João da Mata, and he came there and broke one of them, and I broke the other. João da Mata asked Graça what those mugs were and she remained silent. And then he slapped her several times, and she said that those mugs were for her father and mother to come there and eat. And having done this, he ordered her to move the chest aside, and he found there a small bowl with a base and in it some small round sticks, which were whitewashed; *and I heard that Graça had said that it was her God,* though I did not hear it myself because I went away immediately." Margarida had no more to say but begged the scribe to "sign in her place, for she did not know how to sign."[19]

It is tempting to accept testimonies at face value. They are a crucial part of grasping human action, a human story's time and place. But studies in forensic science and law tell us witnesses and protagonists lie, their memories and interests blur, and their views of the action are prone to misinterpretation. Graça knew and did just enough of what was expected of her, and yet her poor grasp of Portuguese and the Catholic liturgy, on one hand, and her communion with ancestors and ritual feeding of them, on the other, open up a set of knotted perspectives. How could someone three to four decades under the everyday violence of captivity, monitored and surveilled, her life and labor regimented, not learn the language and theology of her captors? Most telling about the dissonance between Graça's lived experiences and the Christian hegemony of her environment was her *act* of spending "most of her time with black people" in Adena and paying lip service to religious orthodoxy. On this count, her captors were like her, in that Portuguese captains, residents and clergy paid more attention to liquor and so-called mulatto women (like Margarida) than professing their faith. These bureaucrats laboring at the behest of the empire were essential workers who were riddled with contradiction because empires are structures that breed hypocrisy, corruption, and cut-throat politics. The institutions created by empire, including the Inquisition, were not immune to hypocrisy and the like; they merely denied this by claiming their actions were pure and above reproach—no one policed the Inquisition—because Portugal was the empire of god. Graça lived through these hypocrisies, knowing somewhere in her soul that officials of the empire lied when they testified that her case was about truth, justice, and the rule of law.

Pedro Lopes decided on the case, but his determination escalated rather than resolved it. After examining the records and the testimonies he had collected, Lopes ruled indeterminately, "As Graça confessed being a Christian, together with the idols which had been found with her, along with the rest that is shown by the records, this is a criminal case that I cannot determine. I remit these records, along with the imprisoned Graça, to the Bishop of São Tomé, D. Diego Ortiz de Vilhegas, to whom this case pertains because it is in his diocese." "I beg Captain Manuel de Albuquerque," Lopes wrote, "if he pleases, and on behalf of Holy Mother Church I require him to send under arrest Graça, along with these records, to the Bishop, for him to determine according to justice." The vicar then published Graça's sentence in São Jorge da Mina on April 14. That day, a scribe delivered the case record to Manuel de Albuquerque, "so he could examine it and decide according to justice."

"Having examined the Vicar's sentence and the quality of the case, as well as what he requires from me on behalf of Holy Mother Church," said Albuquerque, "it seems to me in the service of God and of the King to send this black woman to Portugal to avoid any further impropriety which will not be in the service of Our Lord, for the matter is between black people." With those words, a race was condemned, not merely by an official but for the preservation of the empire. "And therefore," Albuquerque resumed, "I order the *meirinho* [bailiff] of the fortress to deliver Graça under arrest to the captain who comes in the first merchant ship. When he arrives in Portugal, he should consign her, along with these records, to the Judge of the Casa da Índia and Mina (the House of India and Mina) and then remit it to whomsoever it pertains." The factor Barnabé Henriques made a notation in his accounting book, for Graça was a chattel belonging to the king. Albuquerque then published this order where he lived in the fortress on April 20 and ordered all residents of São Jorge da Mina to obey it.

The original records remained with the scribe and the vicar. A copy, written on seven half-sheets, was dispatched with Graça, who was now exiled from homeland and kin, facing another imprisonment and trial. The movement of the sea was unlike anything she had known, for it seemed as though the caravel *Galga*, captained by Rui Dias Freitas, would never reach land. When eventually she was put down in the port of Lisbon, she was then carried off to the Aljube prison, where she waited for what was to come next.[20]

V

It had been a remarkably hot and dry summer in western Europe. It had been so humid, so arid, that rivers disappeared and crops failed. That summer bled into the fall of 1540 when an overseas captive owned by the king of Portugal arrived at the world's busiest seaport. Disembarking after a two-month journey from Africa's Mina (Gold) Coast, she appeared in chains, removed like cargo from the *Galga's* dark hold, under the watchful eye of Captain Freitas. During her passage from the harbor she must have noticed a sample of Lisbon's African population, making up fifteen to twenty per cent of the city's residents, before she was placed in yet another dark hold. Thick walls made the interior of the building look grim. A tense despondency filled the ecclesiastical prison, opposite the Sé Cathedral, the oldest and most iconic church in Lisbon. There in the Aljube, this elderly African woman, baptized Graça, awaited yet another trial in the nerve center of the global empire.

With the core imperial institutions of empire, the nerve cells, being connected through belief, Graça must have struck a blow against them, as she was accused of crimes against Catholicism. Saddled with the borderline charge of witchcraft, she sat in a small cell with no lights or visitors, except clerical and senior people. Jailor António Feio de Castelhaco and his wife, Caterina da Fonseca, were instructed to have no communication with her.

Prisoners paid for their own support, for food, drink, and medical care, with family or personal assets. For the enslaved, that responsibility fell on their holders, and thus officials tried to avoid jailing abandoned captives. Without support, the poor starved to death or remained at the jailor's mercy. These jailors guarded otherwise unmonitored prisons, locked and unlocked doors and chains, watched how inmates spent their days, and monitored conversations between them. At the time of Graça's incarceration, regulations were issued for inquisitional jailors; these included no communication with inmates or their families and that all inmates be kept in leg irons, except those excused because of illness or very old age. Graça fell in the latter category.[21]

With her parents deceased and counted among the ancestors, and her children and grandchild still in Africa, Graça had little more than memory to comfort her as the prison's darkness fell upon her. Graça was also burdened by the way gender shaped criminality and empire: monarchs advised court judges to spare male prisoners who were needed for imperial expansion, for these men were more useful alive than dead as sailors, soldiers, and colonizers. If, as one clergyman described it, the Aljube of Lisbon was "a tomb for the dead," then Graça was not only kinless. She was destined for a fate far worse than that of her deceased parents—to die alone in her slaver's land without the possibility of returning home for a proper burial. Without proper burial, she might not culturally register among her ancestors, for she could not go home. Graça faced, then, the real possibility of an irrevocable alienation that would become a fixture in the lives of millions evicted from modern notions of humanity (as "slaves") and their homelands.[22]

Aljube, from the Arabic al-jabb, meaning a cistern or deep dungeon, was the name of the prisons in a series of trading posts constituting the Portuguese empire. Prisons named Aljube existed in Évora, central Portugal, in Rio de Janeiro, southeast

Brazil, and in Goa, southwest India. They served a tribunal in each locale, connected like dots across the globe but subordinate to the Lisbon tribunal. Lisbon served as the capital of Portugal as well as its far-flung empire. While Lisbon was open to the "new" worlds encountered, it closed in on its own population through a set of inquisitional structures and prisons, thereby transforming itself into a captive city. The rise in incarceration and captivity were coterminous, for once the Inquisition was established, it had to create a network of prisons and cooperating institutions, requiring the reorganization of urban space in a globalized city. In Lisbon, the monarch wielded the Inquisition as a new and powerful weapon to defend and disseminate ortho-doxy, through an anti-Islamic defensive posture, and through repurposing doctrinal institutions such as the College for the Doctrine of the Faith and, later, the House of Catechumens.[23]

The Lisbon tribunal had authority over Brazil, Portugal's Atlantic islands, and Africa, unlike the Spanish Inquisition, which set up tribunals in Lima, Mexico City, and Cartagena. But the Portuguese empire began to take decisive shape in the 1530s when trading enclaves morphed into colonies of sorts. Goa became the capital of Portuguese Asia in the Eastern Hemisphere, and then Brazil received its first permanent settle-ment, followed by colonization, in the Western Hemisphere. Situated between these hemispheres was Africa, with no tribunal, no Aljube. The monarchy in Lisbon had a solution for its trad-ing posts in Africa: in areas under its authority, accused heretics were exported to Lisbon to stand trial. If the Portuguese Inquisition, established in 1536, was the face of the empire, then nonconformity to its prescriptions created enemies of the impe-rium. Like warships or armies, the presence of nonconformist individuals threatened the claims of religious purity and ortho-doxy that stood at the heart of the empire and ran through its institutional arteries. Anonymous denouncements of both nationals and colonial subjects served to protect the empire's underbelly, or so the Inquisition, the empire's immune system, led the monarchy to believe.[24]

Emanating from the empire's capital into the Atlantic and Indian oceans, the Aljubes and secular courts and prisons formed an ensemble orchestrated by the Portuguese Crown and its handpicked Grand Inquisitor, resulting in a wide net of fear and coercion cast over homebound souls and foreign subjects. The Inquisition policed belief and moral behavior in the empire, and any real or imagined threat to it faced punishment or, worse, death. Though inquisitional officials oversaw the tortures used to extract confessions, they transferred the execution of sentences to secular officials, especially killings. This way, blood on their inquisitional hands was removed and purity preserved. The close liaison between the monarchy, bishops, and inquisitors with their own courts and prisons made the partnership between them and the secular courts and prisons a seamless one. That partnership allowed the Inquisition to work in concert with bishops and religious orders. And, so, Lisbon's secular prison, called the Limoeiro, occupying a large, irregular building that had once served as a palace, was right next door to the Aljube. The Limoeiro's single building consisted of six jails; around the time of Graça's trial, these housed between five hundred and a thousand inmates, each divided by gender. The Limoeiro and the Aljube buildings stood side by side, with courthouses on the upper floors, ordinary prisoners on the lower levels, and noble inmates on the top of each edifice.[25]

On September 15, Captain Freitas appeared at the home of Diego Ortiz de Vilhegas, bishop of São Tomé and Mina, on Saco Street. Having just arrived from Mina, Freitas presented the records of Graça's criminal case to Bishop Vilhegas, based on Vicar Lopes's interrogations. A representative of the bishop at the fortress church, Lopes was responsible for maintaining the host and baptismal font, hearing confessions, ministering to the garrison, presiding over burials, converting Africans bordering the fortress, and preparing annual lists of Portuguese and African parishioners. Lopes had given Freitas the records and asked that he deliver them sealed and unopened upon arrival in Lisbon. Vilhegas ordered his scribe to open them and read them aloud. Lopes consigned the case to Vilhegas because he had ecclesiastical authority over the Portuguese colony of São Tomé and the Portuguese fortresses-cum-trading posts on the Mina (Gold) Coast. The records were then taken to members of the Court of Appeals, who, observing "their quality and how they are made concerning the arrest of Graça on matters of faith, ruled Graça be imprisoned as she was consigned." The former rector of the University of Coimbra, where the elites of the empire were educated, Dr. Álvaro Esteves served on the king's High Court of Justice and as magistrate of Guinea. On September 17, he published his ruling at his Lisbon home "because the Court was on vacation, and no hearings took place."[26]

Graça was the earliest of all inquisitional prisoners from Africa. The first public ceremony for the punishment of heretics, called the *auto-da-fé*, or trial of faith, took place in Lisbon on Sunday, September 20, 1540. Assisted by King João III, the senior inquisitor João de Melo presided over the spectacle, demonstrating the authority over life and death which the new Inquisition wielded. Melo would soon become involved in Graça's case, after she entered Lisbon, then the Aljube on Wednesday, September 16. The Inquisition, which is to say the empire to which it was tethered, was still becoming organized, elaborating its regulatory procedures and protocols for both home and abroad. Though the Inquisition originated in 1536, its first general regulations did not appear until 1552. That year, further regulations for the College for the Doctrine of the Faith were issued. The papal bull authorizing the creation of Portugal's

Inquisition declared that for the first three years civil procedures should be followed, and for the first decade no sentences could involve property confiscation. And so no official list of inquisitional victims has survived for the first decade, while the Inquisition was under monarchical control. And then there is Graça and her slender dossier. For what her case lacks in detail, it makes up for in timing and perspective.[27]

VI

Vilhegas was a Castilian priest and theologian who served Portuguese monarchs on matters of astronomy and navigation, tutoring João III, architect of Portugal's Inquisition. Vilhegas was appointed bishop of São Tomé, and then bishop of Ceuta during Graça's trial. It was to his residence that Gaspar Tibão brought Graça, who had been processed at the Casa da Mina. Tibão was one of several treasurers at the Casa da Mina, which was located on the ground floor of the Ribeira Palace on the Lisbon waterfront; it was the agency where commodities arriving from Mina were unloaded and auctioned, and duties collected. Vilhegas then ordered his scribe to take custody of Graça and bring her to the Aljube prison. Her jailors took charge, escorted her to a cell, and pledged not to release her without a warrant from Vilhegas.[28] A few days later, Graça was retrieved from the Aljube and brought again to the home of Vilhegas, but this time to be interrogated with "many questions that were due in the name of justice."

After she was transported from prison to Vilhegas's residence under arrest, the bishop began questioning Graça, prodding her memory as she was forced to recount earlier parts of her life under captivity. Vilhegas then asked, "Who is your God?" "He was the Lord of all," said Graça, "and He was in the church. I had no more than one God, who is the one that is in the

49

church." Suspicious, Vilhegas probed further: "Is the bowl that was found in your possession your god?" Graça replied, "The bowl was for serving food and it was not god." Since her case concerned idolatry and sorcery, Vilhegas asked, "Are the sticks which were in the bowl intended for casting spells?" Graça said, "No," then explained, "a grandson of mine named Martinho had placed them in the bowl to play with them." "Do you know how to cast spells?" "No," she said, "I believe in God and the Virgin Mary, and I renounce the Devil."

Vilhegas's questioning was not over. He continued, asking, "Is Jesus Christ the son of Our Lady the Virgin Mary?" Graça said, "I do not know. Neither the priest nor my godparents ever taught me such a thing." The bishop stopped. He ordered that his scribe produce a written record of his questions and her responses. These were collated with the records from Mina, and taking them together the bishop ordered his scribe "to prepare this case with them." Prominent in Vilhegas's mind was the "quality of the faults of the imprisoned defendant Graça," and having examined them, he ordered "the prosecutor to proffer the charges against her at the first hearing. And that the King's attorney is notified to defend Graça since she does belong to the King."[29]

On September 24, when Vilhegas officially relinquished his role as bishop of São Tomé and Mina, though he would remain on the case, the prosecutor Manuel Manriques, arguing on behalf of the Inquisition, received the records. Manriques took only three days to review the case records and present his charges. As Graça sat in the Aljube, pondering her fate in darkness, Manriques made his case to the bishop in several arguments. Manriques spoke: "I seek to prove that, since Graça is a Christian who had received the water of the Holy Sacrament of Baptism in the city of São Jorge da Mina, the said Graça, oblivious of our Holy Catholic Faith, did not perform the acts of a true Christian or take care to know the Pater Noster, Ave Maria, Creed, or Salve Regina as she was obliged. Rather, she was oblivious to everything. With little fear and reverence towards the Lord God, she made idols, kept them and worshipped them, and cast spells and had them hidden in her house. And because of this, she was publicly defamed, and there was much public voice and rumor against her, in the city of São Jorge da Mina, where she lived."

The prosecutor continued, "I also seek to prove that, while insisting on Graça's persistent determination and treachery, on April 7, 1540, in the São Jorge da Mina fortress, in the oven-house and lodgings of Graça, there were found with her certain idols. Namely, a small bowl the size of a small plate, and inside it four round sticks four fingers long, all of them covered with flour or whitewashed to become whitened. When Graça was asked about this, she replied that it was her God, which she worshipped. And after a while, after being asked by someone else about it, she again said with arrogance and great obstinacy that it was her God, making it clear that she believed in it and held to it. She kept a clouded face whenever people doubted it, and she held it without any doubt, that they were, for she considered them to be, idols."

"I will prove that," Manriques added, "on the day and place mentioned above, there were spells found with her, contrivances and materials to make them. Namely, two clay mugs between two chests, namely, one mug and the bottom of another, both fixed to the floor with clay, and in them feathers mixed with something disgusting, like porridge. And when asked about these, she replied that it was for her father and mother to eat from, as they would eventually come there to eat, her father and mother having been deceased a great many years ago from this worldly life. Graça believed, as a bad Christian and infidel, that they would come, and as an idolater, she believed in and worshipped the idols, saying at night heathen and idolatrous prayers over the said mugs."

Manriques brought his case to a close, reiterating, "I seek to prove that Graça stubbornly persisted in her evil customs and did not seek to learn about our Holy Faith, as she is obliged. When asked whether Jesus Christ, Our Savior, was the son of the Virgin Mary, she replied that she did not know, as someone who took little care of knowing the matters of Faith, necessary to the salvation of her soul, instead of doing the opposite in everything. For this reason, and for what was said above, she deserves to be severely punished. Of this, there is the support of public opinion. Considering what has been said, I ask that she be sentenced to the penalty she deserves by law and to pay the legal costs."

On September 27, Manriques's charges and the related records were brought to the attorney of the king's cases at the Casa da Mina. Manriques told the king's attorney to come with his arguments to the second hearing, as ordered by Bishop Vilhegas. Graça's attorney met with her and began to craft her defense. But would it be enough to convince the bishop and the inquisitors? Might this be the opportunity for the exercise of justice that Vilhegas talked about?[30]

VII

On October 5, the king's attorney, an unnamed individual, presented counterarguments on behalf of Graça. The hearing took place at Vilhegas's residence. Before launching into his arguments, the king's attorney complained to Vilhegas, "Of this case, I do not have any information, except what is contained in these records, as this slave only now came to Portugal. Therefore, the case is such that nothing more should be said, but only that justice be done." Vilhegas concurred. Before proceeding, he asked that Graça supply information to the king's attorney, who said, "Because I have no information I will not contest." This way, Vilhegas reasoned, the king's attorney would be able to present his objections at the second hearing. In turn, the bishop's scribe notified Graça of the bishop's order and read it to her. He said, "You are to instruct someone to provide information to the king's attorney, who will be your attorney." Graça replied, "I have no one to do it on my behalf." She asked the bishop to decide her case. The king's attorney was then allowed to visit Graça in prison and obtain her statement, for, as Graça admitted, "I had no one to send it through." With her statement in hand, she thought "he would be able to bring his contestation to the second hearing."

More than a week passed before the king's attorney presented his objections and laid out his counter-case. "Contesting," said the king's attorney, "and that it be done: I seek to prove that Graça, the king's slave, is about sixty to seventy years old, a woman of little knowledge and a newly arrived *boçal* [slave], unable to speak Portuguese except in the manner of a newly arrived black woman, for the most that she understands is by gestures and pointing to things, so that through them she can understand what is said to her."

"The reason for this," he explained, "is that Graça lived in Mina, without ever coming to Portugal, and spent most of her time with black people, with whom she talked. Therefore, it is only to be expected that she should not have enough [religious] instruction to know and do what is required by justice." Once enslaved by the Portuguese, and laboring in the Mina fortress, Graça had existed in a liminal space. She belonged neither to the fortress community of her captors nor to the village of her friends and extended family. That she spent much of her time in Adena, engrossed in the language and cultural forms there, says something about Graça's commitments and her desire for community and real connections. Though enslaved in São Jorge, she gives the impression of having been liberated on each trip to Adena, with each conversation with local people, each taste of indigenous food. It seems that her bonds with the villagers more so than with the fortress residents had made her vulnerable to accusation and denouncement.

The king's attorney launched into his second counterargument. "I seek to prove," he said, "that the accusation against Graça was made by a principal enemy of hers, one João da Mata. He was the supervisor of the oven-house of the castle of São Jorge da Mina, where Graça lived and was a kneader in the said oven-house, baking bread for the people." Pressing Graça's case, the king's attorney charged, "And thus João da Mata, being the oven-house's supervisor, *entered into conversation* with a mulatto woman by the name of Margarida, who lived in São Jorge da Mina. Having entered into the said conversation with her, he contrived to place Margarida to work in the oven-house and to put Graça out." Though Portuguese officials did their best to scrub details about intimacy from their records, the phrase "entered into conversation" has undoubted sexual connotations, especially in the context of the gendered relations between superiors and subordinates, such as existed between João da Mata and Margarida Rodrigues. Their association had implications.

João da Mata's lover, Margarida, had a son in 1519 and had worked in the oven-house and known Graça from the time she began there, if not earlier. Portuguese men hoisted high their devotion to the Christian principle of monogamy when remarking on African polygamy or intimate relationships among Africans, and yet they themselves were extremely promiscuous with African and "mulatto" women, ignoring the fact that for African rulers polygamy was often a political decision and that adultery among Africans was severely punished. A few years after Graça's trial, Vicar Gonçalo Toscano de Almeida wrote to João III, complaining about "fifteen manumitted black women, who were your slaves and now are free at the expense of the property and salaries of the poor residents, and with whom these and some of your officers live so dishonestly and publicly as if they were their lawful wives, the residents being married in Portugal, with wife and children, of whom they are very unmindful." Though Almeida noted "the men live in sin and participate in this concubinage," insinuating that "this city will become a second Sodom and Gomorrah," he ultimately blamed the women, pleading that "these manumitted black women [be sent] to the Kingdom or to São Tomé, because ... they are harmful to the lives of men," since in the two years he had spent at Mina "six or seven men have died solely as a result of going after these black women." The offspring of Graça, Margarida, and so many others might indicate a collective and serial form of rape, and yet survival in this imperial harem did not necessarily mean community among the women in spite of their shared experience of sexual violence.[31]

And so, Margarida, "speaking against Graça," the king's attorney continued, "said that she was a witch and that she had made the contrivances of the bowl and everything else of which she is now accused. It was all a set-up by Margarida together with João da Mata. They took the sticks which a grandson of Graça used to play a children's game, similar to tipcat (played with sticks with tapered ends), and put them in the bowl and then immediately went to the priest to make their accusation. All of this to expel Graça and place Margarida in the oven-house, as in fact happened. Today, Margarida is there, working in the oven-house. I ask that this being so, no proceedings are taken against Graça in any respect."

In his closing argument, the king's attorney said, "I seek to prove that Graça, our King's slave, is a good Christian, and because she knows the acts of a Christian, she did all she could. However, being a newly arrived slave and not knowing how to speak our tongue, she was unable to learn the prayers that every faithful

Christian is obliged to know. Yet, in all she could do, she has always attended the church in the São Jorge da Mina castle, both on Sundays and on the other days whose observance the Holy Church commands, and on the other days when the Divine Office was celebrated, she was soon in the church. And with her heart and external acts, she performed and showed that she was a Christian, and did whatever she could; because of her tongue, she was not and is not able to know and learn anything else. Therefore, in everything, Graça has no guilt for which she should be punished in the face of all that is alleged against her. Absolution requested." "I request," added the king's attorney, "that it be admitted. And if proved, that she may be acquitted."[32]

VIII

October 14 came. Bishop Vilhegas acknowledged receipt of the counterarguments offered by the king's attorney as well as his plea for Graça's acquittal and pardon. Prosecutor Manuel Manriques was then told that if he had any rebuttal, he should bring it. Vilhegas's scribe "took the case records to the prosecutor so that he could present his reply against the defendant, Graça, at the hearing." Five days passed. Then, Manriques appeared at the bishop's house and said, "I have no reply." He, instead, asked the bishop to assign a term of proof for the charges received and to order that the king's attorney be notified, on behalf of Graça, about the judicial examination conducted in Mina. Vilhegas decided to exempt Manriques from replying and assigned a fifteen-day delay for the parties to present their proof charges and counter-charges.

Vilhegas's scribe went to the king's attorney's home and let him know about the interrogation conducted by Vicar Pedro Lopes at São Jorge da Mina and of the fifteen-day deferment. Regarding the witnesses in these records from Mina, the king's attorney said, "I will bring forward my objections to the witnesses in due time," but as for the term of proof, he said nothing. And then silence fell on Graça's case for days on end, until it was broken at the end of October, when inquisitors held a hearing. Present were Jorge Rodrigues, an inquisitor at the Holy Inquisition's prison, the Aljube, and João da Fonseca, a prosecutor, who had the case records read aloud to him, "so he would come forward with whatever he wanted."

In the Aljube, Fonseca approached his inquisitional superiors at the hearing conducted by Rodrigues and declared, "My lord, the delay assigned to the defendant, Graça, has now been exceeded. Above all, I ask Your Grace to prevent her from presenting any more evidence. And to assign a time limit to coming forward with any objection to the opening and publishing of the court examination." After examining "the quality of the imprisoned defendant's evidence," Rector Giorgius replied, "I grant her ten days to provide evidence for her already delivered contestation."

After this, more time passed. Every second for Graça must have felt as if her sentence had already begun or as if her denouncement ran concurrently with the verdict that made her the king's slave. On November 15, at yet another hearing, this time conducted by Dr. João de Melo, Fonseca raised other concerns. João de Melo, former bishop of the Algarve and later archbishop of Évora, was head of the Inquisition in Lisbon, and was now presiding over Graça's case, as he had at the first *auto-da-fé*, attended by the monarch, the clergy, and all the noblemen. In the Aljube, speaking to Melo, Fonseca stated, "I have examined the case records, and the established terms of this case included summoning the defendant, Graça, and asking her whether she had any objection both to the examinations and to the witnesses." It was ordered that Graça be notified.

And a week later, the king's attorney returned the case records with the following plea, complaining that he had not been informed of the process. "My Lord," he said, "the ten days which were assigned to this imprisoned defendant for reformation were not notified to me. Therefore, I ask Your Grace that they may be granted to me again, for this case still is obscure. News of her, Graça, was sought at the Santa Misericordia [Holy House of Mercy, a charitable organization caring for the sick and poor] from the Bishop of São Tomé in Coimbra, Dom Diego Ortiz de Vilhegas, without anything else being found until now." "This I request," the king's attorney said, "together with the matters in writing." Dr. João de Melo, still in the Aljube, examined the king's attorney's objections but rejected his plea, declaring the interrogations of Graça conducted by Vicar Pedro Lopes formed admissible evidence. The parties were notified, and open to all were the "records concerning Graça, who is imprisoned for being a witch."[33]

On November 9, while Graça sat in the Aljube, Cosme Dias entered the prison. He was an examiner of the customs house's judge. Dias came to the Aljube not to further interrogate Graça but to pry whatever incriminating details he could from her jailors, António Feio de Castelhaco and his wife, Caterina da Fonseca. Potentially, those awaiting trial in the Aljube might collaborate with other prisoners in devising their stories, or their strategy, before reaching the inquisitional judges. Prisons, then, were engineered with peepholes for guards like António and Caterina to surveil and regulate activities in the cells. Spying generated information that could be used to bring added charges or reinforce existing ones.

Castelhaco was asked the customary questions but said nothing. Afterward, he was asked "about the first article of the contestation of the defendant, Graça, which had been read in its entirety and declared to her in detail." To this, Castelhaco said, "It is true that the defendant is in prison and, judging by her looks, seems to be about sixty years old. She understands and speaks our language very poorly, and, when she came here under arrest, they told me that she came from Mina and that she had been a Christian there." He said no more. When asked about the second article of the contestation, he said nothing. To the third, he said, "The only thing I know is that, since this slave has been in prison in my custody, I have seen her commend herself to God and comport herself like a Christian." Concerning the other articles, he said no more.

Dias then turned his attention to Castelhaco's wife. Like her husband, Fonseca said nothing in answer to the customary questions, and she confirmed Graça had been in the Aljube for about two months. "The said slave, Graça, seems to me," said Fonseca, "to be a woman of about sixty years old, and she is a newly arrived black woman who understands little and speaks our language even worse." Dias then asked her about the second article. She said, "I only know that, when the imprisoned defendant arrived here, people said that she came from Mina." As for the third article of Graça's contestation, "which had all been read in its entirety and declared to her in detail," Fonseca said, "It is true that, since this defendant has been imprisoned in this jail, I saw her performing the acts of a Christian. One day, probably about a month ago, in the morning, when I was in a place where this black woman could not see me, and there was no one present with the defendant, I saw her kneeling and lifting her hands while commending herself to God, raising her eyes to the sky, whence it seemed to me the defendant was a good Christian. And this is all I know and nothing more." As regards the other articles, she chose to respond with silence.

When it seemed no one else would be called as a witness, Dias had a surprise. He swore in one Álvaro Gonçalves, a retainer of Manuel de Albuquerque. Albuquerque and his servant had returned from São Jorge da Mina after Captain António de Miranda de Azevedo replaced Albuquerque. In step with earlier witnesses, Gonçalves said nothing in response to the customary questions. When asked "about the first article of the defendant's contestation, which had been read in its entirety and declared to him in detail, he said it is true that he had been in Mina acting as a supervisor for Manuel de Albuquerque." At that time, he said, "This slave, Graça, was in Mina and served in the kneading-house. Of her age, I do not know it, only that she is very old and does not speak as well as the slaves of Lisbon." He had nothing more to add. Concerning the second article, he said, "It is true that João da Mata was supervisor of the oven-house of Mina, and that the defendant belonged to the King and also worked in the kneading-house where she kneaded the dough. I indeed saw João da Mata complaining about this slave being a bad servant; whether for this reason João da Mata bore ill will against the defendant, I do not know." In response to the third article, Gonçalves said, "Several times I saw Graça going to church and praying while kneeling and lifting her hands as if she was commending herself to God, and this took place in the church at Mina."

If Gonçalves was the last witness, it is odd that Manuel de Albuquerque, as captain of Mina, did not testify or was not called to testify. Even stranger, none of Graça's family, including her grandson Martinho, were called to testify either in Mina or in Lisbon. There was no advantage for the Inquisition in summoning kin from Mina or Adena villagers with whom Graça spent more of her time. And yet, if the vicar Pedro Lopes was interested in justice—a clarion call for the empire—then he could have examined the kin and local peoples who knew Graça. Lopes and his Lisbon superiors chose not to exercise that possibility.[34]

IX

There were no further testimonies. The extant testimonials were then given to the prosecutor Manuel Manriques for his response. December 1 came and, with it, Manriques's arguments. "My

Lord," he pronounced, "the defendant did not contest the charges. Everything contained in the charges is clearly proved, because, as confessed by the defendant, in the questions which were asked of her, it is stated that she did not know the Pater Noster nor the Ave Maria nor the Creed. Not knowing the Creed, she could not be a good Christian, for she ignored the articles of Faith."

"She also said she did not know whether Our Redeemer, Jesus Christ, was the son of Our Lady, the Holy Virgin Mary," Manriques argued, "which the defendant and every Christian are obliged to know. This is one of the main articles of our Holy Catholic Faith." The prosecutor reasoned, "If someone uncertain in matters of Faith is an infidel, all the more so is one who is ignorant of them. And, further, it is proved that she had with her some small round sticks, covered with flour or whitewashed, placed in a small bowl. The defendant said they were her God, which she worshipped, and she was an idolater despite being a Christian and having received the water of Holy Baptism, as she confessed. And she had two mugs which were behind some chests, with porridge or something of the kind, and said that her father and mother come there to eat, which was a heathen superstition. There is no doubt that she is a renegade from the Catholic Faith and should, therefore, be severely punished, which I request, with costs."

On December 9, it was now time for the king's attorney to respond. He reminded the hearing that when Graça was baptized, there was no one in São Jorge da Mina to instruct her further, "because she had no master in Mina for she belonged to the King." He recounted her troubles with her denouncer, João da Mata, and said that, although "she is a black woman and newly arrived and does not speak Portuguese well," she was "quick-witted enough to know what is required to be a Christian, and so the questions which were asked in Mina, she answered them based on what she knew, being a person of little knowledge and newly arrived." The king's attorney, in closing, pleaded on the grounds of "ignorance of the law and lack of malice in any transgression" that Graça, "being a black slave from Guinea who had never come to Portugal to be thus instructed in the Faith," be acquitted, with costs awarded to her.[35]

X

The inquisitors were ready for a decision. Whether Graça was present or absent made little difference to the outcome. What mattered was the process of delivering justice for the empire. It involved no small cost or effort to uproot an elderly woman, transport her over two thousand nautical miles to Lisbon, and lock her in prison for a borderline transgression. She, so the inquisitors and her denouncers reasoned, must have done something to strike back at the empire which had enslaved and then imprisoned her. The case offered by the king's attorney on Graça's behalf was strong: an enslaved and illiterate African woman who had never been to Portugal nor truly learned Catholic orthodoxy or the Portuguese language should be granted leniency and acquitted of all charges. But senior inquisitor João de Melo and other officials declared, "We sentence the defendant to life imprisonment, where she will be instructed in the Faith. We assign her as her prison the Monastery of Santa Clara of this city of Lisbon, and we charge in conscience the Mother Abbess and nuns of the monastery with taking very great care in her instruction and salvation." Their ruling was signed and published on December 22, 1540.[36]

Immediately after the ruling, Graça was removed from one prison and delivered to another, to serve her life sentence. Female and male convicts sentenced to carceral church institutions were separated by gender. The same was true for the Aljube. Abbeys and convents often had their own private prisons, and so there might have been one that Graça joined at the Santa Clara monastery. A decade after Graça's forced admission to the monastery, an eyewitness described the convent in this way: "The Santa Clara Monastery is on the outskirts of the city. And it consists of observant nuns of the order of St. Clare. And there are a hundred nuns, who have certain obligations of Masses for the income given to them from São Francisco when the observance was changed. There are two chapels for daily Mass sung by clerics, and an Ascension fraternity run by laity and nuns. The alms of this brotherhood are worth eighty *cruzados*. And the monastery rent is worth twelve hundred and fifty *cruzados*. It has twenty-five servants inside and outside." The nuns at Santa Clara received Graça in this establishment, subsidized by imperial belief and slavery, and made necessary by rupture and kinlessness.[37]

From baptism to baking bread, Graça was pulled into the orbit of Atlantic commerce through a missionary and slaving empire that struck gold in her homeland. Whether by coincidence, by luck, or as part of the general forces of human history, Graça was to be discarded as yet another inquisitional victim of the nascent empire and then forgotten as an African, a woman, and an enslaved person. And yet the same institutions, the same bureaucratic instruments created by the empire to prop itself up and silence threats to orthodoxy, created its undoing. Casting Graça away could not and did not halt the practices for which she was accused. They increased with more boldness because indigenes on the Mina (Gold) Coast knew that the Portuguese were a force to be reckoned with on the high seas but that they had little power on land. And the land was theirs—the same land where ancestral forces lay, the same land from which Graça was evicted. In so many ways, her story underscores the volatility, the fragility, the wars of captivity and belief, and the condemnation of other "races" that were woven into the European project for modernizing the world in their image. If Graça was condemned to a life sentence and jailed in a monastery, then so too were

African peoples and their embodiment of her cultural values, ideas, and forms.

Over eight months of denouncement, detention, and interrogation came to a legal but not an existential end when Graça's sentence was pronounced. The daughter who matured into the woman who became the "king's slave" was now a perpetual prisoner of the Catholic god and doctrine. Physically unsettled, she was transferred from one ecclesiastical prison to another—Mina's jail, the Aljube, the monastery. Given her old age and the trauma of her trial, Graça probably died at the monastery, without a suitable African burial. That she had a Christian burial is doubtful considering her condemned and spiritually enslaved status. Graça's banishment from her homeland and permanent exile deprived her of the comfort and protection of family and community, personal ties, and the means to connect with kin spiritually. For failing to know what was then common knowledge and practice in Portugal, Graça's life sentence was a death penalty of kinlessness and enslavement to a theology she cared little about, and which cared less about her.[38]

Perpetual incarceration, or life imprisonment, usually lasted three to five years for most inmates given that sentence. Indeed, the vast majority sentenced to institutional confinement only spent a few years in jail. For Graça, the sentence was acutely different. Unlike Portuguese nationals convicted and not sentenced to death by the Inquisition, Graça could never return home. She would never see her family and grandson again. She would never interact with her Adena village friends and extended family. In perpetual incarceration, Graça was still a chattel, so much so that in mid-October 1542 she was recorded as revenue in advance for Pedro da Mota, who was to "make sure whether she has been released and what has become of her. And should he find that she has been released, he shall seize her for His Highness, since she belongs to him."[39]

2

"SHE WAS MANIFESTLY DENYING THE TRUTH"

ɔtorofo de mfe apem tu kwan a, ɔnokwafo de da koro ti no to no.

Whereas the liar takes a thousand years to go on a journey, one who speaks the truth follows and overtakes the liar in a day.

I

ONE DAY DURING THE course of the mid-sixteenth century, in the fortress-city of São Jorge da Mina, a loud quarrel erupted. A heated disagreement between two women spilled over into the public space of the fortress-city, drawing in multiple other "black women". Born in São Jorge da Mina, enslaved and later manumitted, Mónica Fernandes squabbled with Ana Fernandes, described as a "black woman" from Portugal. Mónica and Ana possessed the same surname, yet they were unrelated, sharing only the condition of serving the male Portuguese residents, who outnumbered women in the ratio of eight to one. The source of their argument is not known, for it was not recorded. But whatever it was, it must have been egregious because Ana told Mónica, "If you were in Portugal, I would have someone stab you in the face." And then Mónica swore, while putting her hand on Ana's face: "I would not go to Portugal, but that I would make you cease to be a woman." Days later, Ana fell gravely ill, claiming that Mónica was the cause. Ana's condition worsened: her skin peeled and cracked all over. She then returned to Portugal and succumbed there to her ailment. In Portugal, local physicians told her, just before she died, that her condition was "completely incurable because it was poison." The authorities immediately turned to Mónica as the obvious candidate for perpetrator, but Mónica's involvement turned out to be anything but straightforward. In the course of her trial, she remained unwavering in clinging to her truth while it became clear that her squabble with Ana paled in comparison with the tumultuous times and everyday violence through which she had lived: the tensions between empire, trade, and religious orthodoxy, on the one hand, and the rituals and forms of healing tightly bound to the lived experiences of "all the black men and women in Mina," on the other.[1]

II

The world of Graça persisted in Mónica's time. Though Graça was older than Mónica, they may have known each other, having shared common spaces within and outside the fortress-city. The two also had overlapping experiences, as captives attending to the Portuguese men in São Jorge da Mina. Though both had their births registered in São Jorge da Mina, Mónica spent longer in the fortress-city, for she claimed, "I had always resided in the castle of Mina." There was no fortress when Graça was born, or at least it was then under construction. As the parents and relatives of both women were non-Christian, Mónica was thus a baptismal name. How she came to reside in the fortress-city is an open question which we have no evidence to answer. However, she appears to have been taken into the world of São Jorge da Mina rather than conceived there, because "her father and mother had been non-believers in the Christian religion, as well as her other relatives." Graça had a similar background; she even ritually fed her deceased parents' ancestral spirits, keeping their memories and her lines of communication with them alive. Mónica's engagement with a spirituality and set of cultural resources much like Graça's would also lead to her eventual trial and exile. Armed with a poor grasp of the Portuguese language and partial knowledge of Catholic dogma, Mónica would travel a path paved by Graça, and yet their end points were anything but the same.[2]

For all that connected Mónica and Graça, their experiences also differed. Mónica had received her manumission, yet she continued to serve the captain and officials of São Jorge da Mina, washing their clothes and serving in their dwellings. Manumission fell short of freedom, and baptism yoked her to the Christian god and Portugal's king. Ever-present reminders of this twin bondage were her baptismal name and her Portuguese enslaver's tattoo—that of Fernandes. Mónica tells us, "I was a baptized Christian and was baptized in Mina by a clergyman who resided in the fortress and whose name I do not know." That she had been baptized fifteen to twenty years prior to the time of her Lisbon trial places Mónica's entry into the world of Catholicism around 1540, the year Graça's troubles began. Unlike Graça's, Mónica's "godmother was a black woman named Joana Menez," who at the time of her trial resided somewhere in Lisbon but had lived in Mina for some years. "My godfather," said Mónica, "was Lourenço Correia, who lives in Sintra, who used to be a factor in Axim." In 1540–42, the trader Lourenço Correia was indeed stationed at the Portuguese fort of São Antonio near the settlement of Akyem ("Axim"), some eighty miles along the coast to the west.[3] Though no stranger to São Antonio, Mónica spent most of her time frequenting the villages adjacent to São Jorge da Mina, as Graça did, when not working in the fortress-city or on its beaches.

Assuming Mónica was not baptized at birth, she must have received that sacrament in late adolescence since only children— and the enslaved—had godparents at their baptism. Baptism sought to admit Mónica into the Catholic faith, leaving a permanent mark on her soul by erasing her ancestral spirituality. Still, her path to full membership of the Catholic Church remained incomplete, for, as Mónica admitted, "I had not been confirmed." However slender those details, they suggest she was born in the 1520s, during the captaincies stretching from Afonso de Albuquerque (1522–24) to Estêvão da Gama (1529–32), and was baptized at the end of Manuel de Albuquerque's captaincy. As fate would have it, Pedro Lopes, the vicar who initiated charges of witchcraft against Graça, was also the priest who would have baptized Mónica around 1540. Mónica declared, "I confessed every year, except last year [c.1555] because the Vicar of Mina [Diogo Pacheco] did not want me to confess and did not allow me to take the Sacrament," and stated that she "attended Mass every Sunday." And yet how do we explain the charge that "she does not know the Christian doctrine because it had only been taught to her [over] a few days" in September 1556? Was her baptism therefore merely a shallow formal ritual undergone as part of her condition of captivity, or something more?[4]

There was a damning marginal note in her trial records—*não sabe nada da doutrina cristã* ("she knows nothing of Christian doctrine"). Under interrogation, "she crossed herself imperfectly and was unable to say the Pater Noster or the Ave Maria, except for some words from the Pater Noster and others from the Ave Maria, and she did not know any other thing at all about doctrine or the Creed." Mónica, however, had a quick wit. She converted those few days of Catholic catechism into a compelling counter-argument against doctrinal ignorance. When the inquisitor Friar Jerónimo de Azambuja asked "whether she knew who Jesus Christ was, and whose son he was, and whether she knew a man who lay in the church with his arms wide open," Mónica ably replied, "Jesus Christ was Our Lord. He was the one who lay in church with his arms wide open, and I know that he died and was killed by the Jews, and he lived again, and he ascended to Heaven."

Furthermore, she continued, "I know that there is a Day of Judgment and that Our Lord will judge; and I know that there is a Paradise and a Hell and that I do not want to go to Hell but rather to Paradise." Though Mónica stumbled, unable to explain why festive days were celebrated, she "knew that Christians fast during Lent for their sins." Asked if she had any knowledge about Portuguese notions of witchcraft or consulted with witches, or if she had spoken with demons and had become their servant, or if she knew any witches, Mónica declared plainly, "I have never been a witch, and I only at times made some powders, by grinding a broad bean from *my land* with a stick of redwood, and with water and oil, and I anointed myself with it when I was ill."[5] Mónica certainly learned something about Christian doctrine in the face of inquisitional terror. Still, her recourse to therapy in a spiritual culture distinct from that doctrine tells us more about her upbringing and everyday practice.

When Mónica told Friar Azambuja that her land provided medicines for healing, we can be sure she had in mind the region called Mina, as her medicine was "a thing which her fellow natives [speaking Portuguese] call *feitiços* and was forbidden by the Vicar." *Feitiços* referred to "magic" and "sorcery" in Portuguese, with the connotation that diverse African objects and practices represented a rival or enemy of Christian doctrine and so equated to sorcery and witchcraft. English "fetish" derives from *feitiço*. *Feitiçaria* called attention to witchcraft in the European sense, with its demonological undertones. With Mónica's spiritual culture on trial, filtered through the Inquisition's demonological preoccupations, these legal procedures were less investigations seeking the truth than a means of enforcing orthodoxy and determining degrees of punishment for heterodoxy. Local Africans or fellow indigenes did not think of their ritual objects and practices in terms of *feitiço* or *feitiçaria*, and neither did Mónica. Rather than seeking out the vicar or acquiring medicines from the Portuguese apothecary, Mónica insisted "that she had been to the local healer of the village which is next to the castle, not to make *feitiços* but to cure herself of a foot which had been bitten by a cat." That village was Adena, the same frequented by Graça before her trials and exile. Asked what this healer did to cure her, Mónica replied,

"He had put something on my foot, I do not know what, and he wet it repeatedly and tied it with a cloth, and this healer was an old black man and was not a Christian." From the head of the Portuguese empire down to its foot soldiers, this testimony was a tremendous slap in the face of its core beliefs, an exposure of the grand hypocrisy of enslaving people in order to save souls, of conducting baptism into captivity and service to men of the empire. The friar was infuriated. He lashed out and told Mónica that "she was manifestly denying the truth!" But was she? Or was her truth his and the global empire's lie?[6]

III

Maria Domingues arrived at the São Jorge da Mina fortress in 1542. Maria claimed that, during the captaincy of Francisco Pereira (1532–36?), Mónica Fernandes had quarreled with Ana Fernandes, "a woman who had been brought from the Kingdom by the said Francisco Pereira to serve him." Ana threatened Mónica: "If you were in Portugal, you would pay for it." Mónica pushed Ana in her face, telling her that "she would cast a spell upon her so that she would never be a woman again." At least that is what Maria had heard about the moment. From that time onward, Ana and Mónica argued with each other. Maria said, "I had always heard that a black woman named Mónica Fernandes, who had been manumitted, made use of *feitiços*." According to Maria, Ana Fernandes "always scratched herself greatly and complained of the said Mónica Fernandes." Maria saw Ana with "her face all peeled off and very cracked, and she died of it." Since Mónica's trial at São Jorge da Mina would not commence until a decade later, before she was exiled to Portugal another four years after that, her confrontation with Ana Fernandes was not the precipitating event. Instead, her accusers believed that a whole series of stories involving Mónica revealed a pattern of misdeeds on her part that lay at the heart of the charges against her.[7]

Described as "a manumitted slave [that] used to belong to Our Lord the King," that is, João III, another witness, Clara, confirmed that during the captaincy of Francisco Pereira, a time when João III acquired the Spice Islands that are now part of Indonesia and approved the Portuguese settlement of Brazil, Mónica quarreled with Ana, "a woman who had been brought from Portugal by the said Francisco Pereira." Among other things, Clara heard that Mónica had sworn "by Ana's face that she would cast upon her such a spell that she would never again be a woman." Even if we cannot fully understand what was meant by the phrase "never again be a woman," Ana was not ever the same again. Days later, Clara saw Ana "all peeled off and with her face very badly treated, complaining that Mónica had killed her." Later, Clara heard that Ana had died of that condition in Portugal.[8]

Maria, Clara, and, later, Marta and Catarina all confirmed that Ana had confronted and threatened Mónica. But none actually witnessed what they heard. Only Margarida de Albuquerque, yet another manumitted woman of African ancestry, "at the time Mónica Fernandes had quarreled with Ana Fernandes ... had seen them quarrel with each other." Through Margarida's eyes and ears, we learn that "among other words proffered by both, Ana Fernandes said to Mónica Fernandes that, if she were in Portugal, she would have someone stab her in the face. And that Mónica Fernandes had sworn, while putting her hand on her face, that she would not go to Portugal, but that she would make Ana Fernandes cease to be a woman." It was Margarida who was the source of the other women's gossip. Just as had been foretold, Ana soon fell ill, complaining that Mónica had set in motion the process of killing her. She later died in Portugal, where physicians pronounced that her incurable illness was caused by poison, not sorcery. And so, starting from this incident, rumors began to spread. Women like Catarina, also known as Madu, could only say it was "rumored that Mónica Fernandes had killed here Ana Fernandes, and that she was now likewise planning to kill another woman, and that for that purpose she was going to the village to take advice from indigenous healers."[9]

In her time at the fortress-city, Maria had "heard many black women of this fortress say that, in the salt village, Mónica Fernandes had a pot in which she kept the names of all the captains and officials and gentlemen, saying in those ceremonies that they should all be for her, and do her good, and favor her, and not send her to Portugal." One of those women was Marta Fernandes, who also heard that Mónica "had a pot with charms in the salt village and that she sometimes went there to perform her ceremonies in the said pot; and that she uttered the names of the captains, and officials, and other men, from whom she wished to receive favor." Salt-producing villages existed to the immediate east of Adena and São Jorge da Mina in Akatakyi and to the west in Fetu. Whether or not Mónica performed rituals involving a pot to gain the Portuguese men's favor, her manumission had come about from years of serving these same men. The pot, either an earthen vessel called kukuwa or the brass variety called kuduo, served culinary and ritual purposes. Marta Fernandes, another manumitted woman of African ancestry, knew the rumors circulating in the fortress-city. Because she and Mónica did not speak to each other, whatever Marta understood came from hearsay. Around 1543–44, Marta heard that Mónica "made use of sorcery and that she always went to the village [Adena] to talk to the female healers." If Mónica possessed a ritually treated pot or vessel called asuo yaa, which female healers and spiritualists used to perform divination, why would she then consult a male healer to harm another woman? Why not make the spiritual inquiry and carry out the suspected harm herself?[10]

In early to mid-August 1552, so Maria understood, Mónica traveled to the Aguada near the salt village on the way to Fetu.

Though *aguada* referred to water in a ship's tanks or casks, it also signaled the places where supplies were obtained from fountains or springs along the coast. As Portuguese ships needed water supplies, places to secure water were carefully marked on maps and in sailing instructions as ports of call. This Aguada was located between Adena and Fetu, and it was there, according to Maria, that Mónica "had sent for a healer and told him to consult with his spiritual force [called an *ɔbosom*] whether Lucrécia Correia, a manumitted black woman whom the *meirinho* Bento Roiz had brought from Portugal, was a *bruxa* ['witch']." The male healer answered that she was not. Furthermore, he said, "Lucrécia Correia was wild but not wicked in any other way."[11]

Days or a week later, Mónica washed the captain's clothes at the Aguada and hung them out to dry. The manumitted woman Clara saw Mónica "carrying a bowl in her hand and watering the said clothes, and she blew towards the fortress and the black people's side," which is to say the nearby African settlements. Clara indicated that Catarina, "a slave of Our Lord the King, also known as Madu, had spied on Mónica deliberately and crossed herself, saying 'I renounce the Devil'." In a deferential voice, Madu said, "I knew nothing about this case except that, once when we were both in the Aguada, I had seen that Mónica Fernandes was carrying a basket in her hand with *feitiços*, and that she put her hand in the basket, and that she anointed herself, that is, her face, feet, arms, and breasts, and after she had done this she spread the contents of the basket over the clothes, and she blew in all directions. And that, when I had seen this, I blessed myself and said to me, 'Jesus, I renounce the Devil,' and that from then onwards Mónica Fernandes had ceased talking to her, though she used to be my friend." As a result of spying on Mónica, Madu may have been left speechless or, as Clara and others testified, unable to speak, with the suggestion that Mónica or her alleged rituals were to blame. However,

Madu's testimony rebuts the insinuation that she could no longer talk, though she and Mónica were friends no more.[12]

Maria heard that when "Mónica went to wash the Captain's clothes, she wet the clothes with water which the said healer blessed for her while performing his ceremonies." Clara also heard or came to understand that Mónica had "gone to the village to the house of a healer, [but] there she had asked him to make her a *feitiço* with which to kill Mesia Fernandes, a manumitted black woman who presently serves in this fortress as a woman of the kneading-house." The same healer, according to Clara, told Mónica that Mesia "could not die because she was not guilty of anything, and that, since the *feitiço* was already made, she should give him a chicken and a yam, in order that he could undo the ritual so that the said Mesia Fernandes should not die." Had Mónica refused to provide the yam and the chicken, alleged Clara, "he would have exposed Mónica Fernandes since he was friends with Mesia Fernandes, and he did not want to see her die." And so Mónica "had straightaway brought him the chicken and the yam, and the chicken had died from certain ceremonies which the healer had performed on it, saying that there went the death of Mesia Fernandes." Consulting a healer did not mean Mónica was not a spiritualist herself. Still, it certainly meant she was conversant with the ideas and practices ascribed to this healer, and the connection between the two suggests they shared lived beliefs, which challenged the Portuguese empire's own beliefs and the Africans under their religious and commercial sway, if not literal captivity.[13]

As if a metaphor for the empire that Mónica and Ana lived under, Ana's return to Portugal and the peeling away of her skin mirrored Portugal's contemporaneous shedding of its burdensome fortresses in North Africa and its recommitment to the Asian spice trade as far as China, while being faced with the increased costs of expansion, indebtedness, and declining state revenue. By the time women like Maria and Clara witnessed or heard about Mónica's deeds, the leading Portuguese gold trading site at São Jorge da Mina and its satellite trading fort at Akyem were adding to the challenges of empire, because they brought in less and less gold—the prime currency of international trade and a buoy to the domestic economy. It is curious but not surprising that João III yielded to these pressures by firming up religious orthodoxy through the Inquisition and ceding to the Jesuits and religious advisors at his court a dominant role in transforming the empire into a commercial and missionary one. The tensions between trade and Christian orthodoxy were palpable, never to be resolved, and Mónica's case underscores why the Jesuits avoided the Mina (Gold) Coast and why Portuguese rule and belief were never firmly planted there, as they would be in Brazil and parts of Asia. That tension found a conduit in the very merchants who claimed adherence to Catholicism but came to Mina precisely because of their stronger passion for gold, captives, and women.[14]

Mónica served not only the captain of São Jorge da Mina but also merchants. One such mercantile agent was Estêvão Soares, a former factor of the fortress-city. Clara indicated that Mónica "served him indoors and that, serving thus, the said Estêvão Soares used to say that he had lost his head over her and that he could not eat or sleep without the said Mónica Fernandes being present." Gonçalo Toscano de Almeida knew Mónica and Estêvão and, in his role as vicar of São Jorge da Mina, he wrote a scathing letter to João III, telling the king about "the many evils and great public sins which exist there and from which ensue great damage and loss both to the property and to the lives of those who live there." Mónica, Clara, Maria, and others were among the "fifteen manumitted black women" whom Almeida targeted as the prime source of such evils and sins. Almeida perhaps had Estêvão Soares or at least his predilection in mind when he informed the king, "Of these black women each of [the men] takes one for himself into his house, and because of [the women] they are ill-treated and offended, which is a great disservice to God and Your Highness and from which many evils follow." If Mónica served men like Soares under the scepter of imperial power, Soares and other male residents tapped into this authority to service their desires and live a kind of freedom unimaginable in Portugal. These men were themselves convicts, exiles, and undesirables. Only captains and the highest-ranking officials came from the ranks of the nobles.[15]

Imperial officials and agents like Soares only paid lip service to official beliefs, offering instead "much opposition" to the vicar's scolding. Waging a losing battle, Almeida was "forced to keep silent." And yet Almeida, steeped in his post and belief, could not ignore the commercial imperative which Soares managed and Mónica served, and which was now threatened by "the French and the pirate ships [that] come to this coast to trade, bringing great trouble to this land, with little benefit to [the empire]." Added to these threats were "the great wars between the black kings within this fortress's jurisdiction, above all those of the big Akan against the small Akan, from which [the empire] derives great loss." These conflicts clogged the flow of gold and goods. And this commerce was the essential condition for the Portuguese presence on the coast, for Mónica's captivity and servile labor, and indeed "there was no larger trade done in this fortress-city of [the empire] than that of these Akan." The fort at Akyem suffered too. Almeida bemoaned the fact that "everywhere the roads are obstructed, together with the great wars waged by a black man whose name is Captain Asa, who has raised himself from nothing and become a thief and a highwayman, so that everyone is afraid of him and pays him a tribute." The damage wrought by Asa and his three hundred armed men prevented local merchants from coming to the Portuguese strongholds at Akyem or São Jorge da Mina. Frustrated by Mónica's unyielding beliefs or by the realization that commerce trumped commitment to faith, Almeida opined, helplessly, "all this trouble and the evils which occur at present were given by God for the sins committed in this land, the public men living in sin." These Portuguese officials and residents, he continued, "mistreat the divine person of God and the saints, and they greatly disobey the Church and its ministers."[16]

Almeida's shaming method yielded few positive results for the orthodoxy that lay at the heart of the empire. To make a public fool of Soares over Mónica, or have Mónica make Soares look like a fool, proved more effective. Clara recalled, "Because he felt so ashamed in front of everyone, he had asked Fernão Gomes, who at that time was Captain, to have her sent to Axim [Akyem] and take her out of his house." Gomes obliged, and Mónica found herself exiled, eighty to ninety miles to the west, in the Portuguese fort at Akyem. But not soon after Mónica arrived there, Soares again asked Fernão Gomes "to have her sent back to him because he was altogether dying from not seeing her." Some like Madu, who spied on Mónica, had come to believe Mónica "had been sent to exile in [Akyem] because it was said that she had cast spells upon Estêvão Soares to make him love her." Marta Fernandes, no apparent relation of Mónica, dismissed that hypothesis and summed the matter up best: "He had lost his head over her, and he was unable to eat or drink without her," and if the captain did not concede and if Mónica did not return to him, "he would die." Rather than placing Soares's desires on trial, the leading theory to explain his erratic behavior pointed to Mónica, for she must have, they reasoned, "administered something to him."[17]

IV

The stream of accusations against Mónica and her ostracism by male residents and women of the fortress-city suggest that Mónica stood alone in facing a crusade against her. This was a drama spiced with spies, friends-turned-enemies, and threats to her face and relative autonomy. In the intrigue that became her case, Mónica did have friends or allies. The healers in Adena and Fetu fit this mold. Within São Jorge da Mina, several women did not or were not called to testify, and shared bonds with her as companions. Though she had no children of her own, she did have a niece who lived in the fortress-city or in one of several neighboring communities. For reasons that will remain unexplained, we hear nothing about or from this niece or her parents. Clara said, "I had heard say that Francisca, a manumitted black woman who served the *Meirinho*, was a companion of Mónica Fernandes." Marta confirmed this friendship between Mónica and Francisca, but the records are silent about Francisca. The same could be said for Lucrécia Correia, who also served the *meirinho* Bento Roiz, and naturally would have known something of their friendship. The absence of male testimony, whether African or Portuguese, is also puzzling. There is an air of selectivity. *How* the empire and its institutions and beliefs presented themselves concealed *what* they were and *why* targeting Mónica was essential to imperial power, especially so far away from the metropolis.

Enslaving commerce and belief—for captives belonged to the Portuguese sovereign and his god—brought Mónica into a global network that was strung together as an empire. Consistency came in slaving and spices and in exporting religion. These tightly interwoven and mutually reinforcing features animated the name Mónica Fernandes—a baptismal name nullifying one anchored in African ancestry, as well as a "slave name" signaling the chattel's trademark. That Marta, Mónica, and her adversary Ana shared the "slave name" Fernandes, and not much else, erodes all assumptions that they might have been kinfolk. In the previous chapter Graça alerted us to this fact of empire and slaving: the possession of a singular first (baptismal) name represented a loss of kin and dispossession because the said person did not own himself or herself. And yet, even if captives had a first and second name, there was still an element of dispossession since a "slave name" registered ownership by another, a mark similar to an iron branding, which inscribed loss of self-proprietorship and natal kinship relations. Since Mónica was born in or around São Jorge da Mina and not Portugal, she and Maria and Ana probably had the same slave-holder. Having known each other in that way, as bonded and then manumitted persons, a particular animus developed between them. It played out along the most prominent fault lines of the empire—Christianity and commerce.

V

Portuguese slavery on African soil, fashioned under the guise of belief, transformed relationships among captives in order to serve the empire. Catarina and Mónica had a relationship. Catarina spied on Mónica, then rebuked her because of a dogmatic belief that Mónica's rituals and healing equated to an engagement in "devilish things." If Mónica's spiritual culture rebuffed the shackles offered by submitting to Portuguese belief, then Mónica's siding with African villagers and healers made her, or, better yet, the ideas and actions she embodied, an immediate threat. But Portuguese officials and clergy could not detect or know such a threat without agents among the women.[18]

Under the spell of an enslaving belief, Catarina, whose pre-baptismal name was Madu, worked on behalf of the empire to identify and eliminate competing beliefs and practices. Mónica's anointing of herself with medicines from the male healer and from villages viewed as the demonic inverse of Portuguese purity of belief made friends into combatants. And so, whatever friendship Catarina and Mónica possessed soon ended, and Mónica "ceased talking to her, though she used to be her friend." Mónica had spotted defects in the architecture of Portuguese slavery in Africa. And yet, the architects had built mechanisms—in the making of an inquisitional empire—whereby orthodoxy seduced, turning Madu into Catarina and Catarina, branded "a slave of Our Lord the King," into a weapon against herself and those like her. When Madu testified against Mónica, she did so "without being given the oath since she was a captive," not realizing she was a pawn and non-member in the community of believers, failing to see the liberation from it all offered by Mónica.[19]

Margarida de Albuquerque, like Madu and Francisca, was also a friend of Mónica. Margarida claimed, "I had always heard say that Mónica Fernandes cast spells; and since I was her friend, I had sometimes rebuked her for it, and [then] Mónica Fernandes had turned away from me and had not spoken to me for many days." When questioned about "what she knew about her at present, though she did not speak with her, [Margarida said] that she bore no ill will against her and that she would tell the truth." During the captaincy of Rui de Melo (c.1552–56), when Mónica faced the vicar's interrogation, Margarida heard from Madu that Mónica had used healers' water to wet the captain's clothes. Using a small basket filled with *feitiços*, Margarida recounted, Mónica had spread them over the clothes and had "blown towards the sea." As Mónica washed clothes or performed these ritual acts, Madu "had sneezed, and blessed herself, and had said to her, 'I renounce the Devil, and wicked women, and witches'." Seeing no other interpretation, Madu disapproved of Mónica's actions. "And from then onwards," Margarida related, "Mónica had ceased talking to her, though they used to be friends."[20]

VI

On September 13, 1552, the newly assigned captain, Rui de Melo, ordered an inquiry by Filipe Eanes, described as the "Vicar of this cathedral of the town of São Jorge da Mina." The inquiry, or

49. Gold Coast fetish object

1. Akan brass-pan "shrine" (left) and *kuduo* (brass vessel) used for divination, c. 1679. (Jean Barbot, *Barbot on Guinea: The Writings of Jean Barbot on West Africa 1678-1712*, eds, Paul Hair, Adam Jones and Robin Law [London: Hakluyt Society, 1992], 2: plate 74, facing p. 580).

2. Three Gold Coast Women, c. 1688. (Jean Barbot, *Description des Côte d'Afrique*, Vol. II., UK NA: PRO, ADM 7/830B, p. 43) [public domain].

3. Lisbon, c. 1572. (Georg Braun and Franz Hogenberg, *Civitates orbis terrarium*, British Library, maps C.7.d.1, vol. 1 (1572), pl. 1]). [public domain].

4. Folio from Graça's trial dossier. (ANTT, Tribunal do Santo Oficio, Inquisição de Lisboa, processo 11041).

5. Convent of Santa Clara. (Wikimedia Commons [https://commons.wiki-media.org/wiki/File:Aerial_photograph_of_Vila_do_Conde_(16).jpg]).

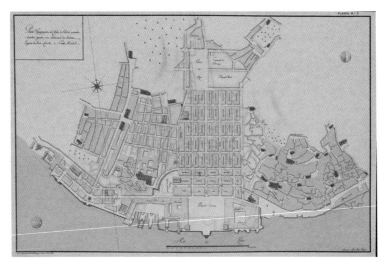

6. Pombaline Baixa, Lisbon, rebuilding plan after the 1755 earthquake by architects Eugénio dos Santos Carvalho and Carlos Mardel (https://en.wikipedia.org/wiki/Lisbon_Baixa#/media/File:Pombaline_Baixa_Lisbon_map_1756.jpg.)

7. São Jorge da Mina and Adena, c. 1572. (Georg Braun and Franz Hogenberg, *Civitates orbis terrarium*, British Library, maps C.7.d.1, vol. 1 (1572), pl. 54]).

8. Inside the courtyard of Elmina. (formerly São Jorge da Mina) fortress today. (Photography © Kwasi Konadu).

9. The ruler of Fetu, a spiritualist healer, and a warrior accompanied by court musicians. (Amsterdam Museum. http://hdl.handle.net/11259/collection.41785).

10. Portuguese fort St. António near Akyem ("Axim"). (Leiden University Libraries. http://hdl.handle.net/1887.1/item:783787.

inquisition, convened in the dwelling of Eanes, examined five women: Maria Domingues, Clara, Marta Fernandes, Margarida de Albuquerque, and Catarina (also known as Madu). Curiously, Mónica evaded the inquiry, but if Graça's case set a precedent, then excluding Mónica remained part of standard procedures. The Inquisition in Lisbon questioned witnesses, spies, and other testifiers, but its officials also interrogated the accused. Since the witnesses in Mónica's case were all "asked about the matters mentioned in this record," one wonders whether their testimonies even mattered, as the witnesses were confined to select women, and each was set up to confirm details provided by those testifying before them. Every witness was called not merely to *tell* what they knew, without hints or prompts, but to *say* something about what was in the record, after the record had first been read to them. Be that as it may, nothing happened after these testimonials were collected. The records were kept on file until three years later.

On July 16, 1555, Francisco Pires, chief *alcaide* (mayor) of São Jorge da Mina, ordered the records and written testimonies in Mónica's case file to be brought to him. Vicar Filipe Eanes had departed from the fortress-city. Pires was informed that Eanes had the records in his possession and that no further steps had been taken on their account. Pires then ordered them delivered to Diogo Pacheco, then vicar of São Jorge da Mina's church, "to do with them as he thought appropriate." Though Eanes had conducted his inquisition in 1552, action on the records remained incomplete "because Rui de Melo, who was Captain at the time, ordered that nothing more be done on their account." Not even the slightest hints exist to suggest, one way or the other, why Rui de Melo sat on an inquiry which he had ordered. Perhaps he knew there was not much there to justify the expense of exiling Mónica yet again, this time to stand trial in Lisbon. Perhaps it was the tenuous nature of his captaincy, fighting off other Europeans who competed for gold and space to operate in an otherwise Portuguese sphere and trade monopoly. Perhaps the rising and unresolved tensions between professions of faith and of Christian orthodoxy and commerce in captives, gold, and spices made Mónica's transgression a matter of minor importance in the larger scheme of things.[21]

A day and a year passed. Days away from his return to Portugal, Rui de Melo allowed the *alcaide* and the new vicar to proceed, reversing an earlier decision not to pursue charges made by Filipe Eanes. Melo's decision while on his way out effectively meant that Mónica's case file was reviewed anew. Vicar Diogo Pacheco's assessment was expected: "These records having been seen, and given that these are crimes and that their cognizance pertains to the Inquisitors, I remit her, Mónica Fernandes, together with the said records, to them, so that they may judge them." As swiftly as Pacheco's determination came, Mónica found herself exiled and aboard a ship bound for Lisbon, following an ocean path crossed less than two decades earlier by Graça. Accompanied by her case file and her unnamed niece, Mónica landed on European soil after two months of sea travel, disembarking in the Atlantic port-city of Lisbon.[22]

VII

Mónica had been exiled before, but this time was different. Condemned and imprisoned, she awaited trial. The uncertainty or fear evoked when Ana threatened to do her bodily harm if she was in Lisbon must have crossed her mind. To be sure, she had no desire to visit Lisbon, home of the Inquisition. In the Palace of Estaus in Lisbon, the official headquarters of the Portuguese Inquisition, Friar Jerónimo de Azambuja received the records on September 1, together with "a black woman named Mónica Fernandes, who declared that she came from Mina under arrest." Both, he declared, were sent to him by Diogo Pacheco, vicar of

Mina. Azambuja had been a royal ambassador to the Council of Trent, which the Catholic Church assembled to respond to the Protestant Reformation in Europe, and he now served as a principal inquisitor with the full title and name of Father Master Friar Jerónimo de Azambuja. Nonetheless, Azambuja turned to Brício Camelo, who oversaw the inquisitional prison, or the Aljube, and ordered him to deliver Mónica to him.[23]

Three days later, in the Holy Inquisition council chamber, "a manumitted black woman named Mónica Fernandes" arrived from the inquisitional prison. There is no way to tell if she sat or stood or lay strapped to some torturous medieval device. Likewise, we have no idea about her state of mind, whether she hoped testifying to the truth would matter, or whether her incarceration had flooded her being with all the things she feared about Portugal. With Mónica's case record to hand, the barrage of questioning began.[24]

Azambuja asked, "Have you done anything to any woman that might have made her skin peel off and her face crack, and finally made her die?" "It is true," Mónica replied, "that, while I was in Mina, I quarreled with a black woman, whose name I cannot recall, and the said black woman came to Portugal." She continued, "When we were quarreling with each other, and the said black woman told me that we would come to Portugal, and she would have my face cut, I told her that she would also have her face cut here. But," Mónica insisted, "I had never cast a spell upon her which would have made her die."[25]

"What was that you carried in the basket and which you used to sprinkle the Captain of Mina's clothes with," asked Azambuja, "and did you blow onto the clothes while you sprinkled it?" Mónica said, "I carried soap in a basket, and I rubbed it on the clothes I washed, but I do not recall blowing onto them, nor did I bring in the basket any *feitiços*." Azambuja moved on, but not in the sequential order of events as laid out in Mónica's case record. He then asked, "What had you done to a certain Soares whom you served, making him incapable of living without having you close to him and, after sending you to [Akyem], to forthwith have you sent back?" With certainty, Mónica said, "I had never cast any spells upon the said Soares. I only served him, and because he was dissatisfied with me, he had the Captain send me to [Akyem], where I stayed for two months. Afterward, the Captain ordered me to return to Mina." Mónica confessed, "I did not want to serve the said Soares, [but] the Captain, who was a certain Fernão Gomes, told me that if I did not serve him again, he would have me whipped." And it was "for this reason," Mónica made clear, "I served him once again, but I never cast any spells upon him."[26]

Azambuja asked "whether in the village you had any pan with the names of the Captain and officials of Mina written down so as to make them love you." Mónica denied the accusation but clarified what her accusers had reported, stating unequivocally, "I never had such a pan, except that, at the time when the male healer had cured my foot, the said healer used to take from a pan the concoction with which he treated me for the cat's bite." Her recorded testimony in Portuguese used the term *mézinha*, a remedy made of a homemade mixture of herbs. Its equivalent would be the English "concoction." In this world of medicine and healing, Azambuja pushed further, asking, "What did you use to anoint yourself with, and what was it for?" Perhaps a bit frustrated, Mónica responded, "I have already said that I anointed myself with the powders made with the broad bean and the stick of redwood to cure myself when I was ill, but that I have never anointed myself with any *feitiços*." Indeed, "this ointment was not made only by me," Mónica explained, "but also by all the black men and women in Mina." If there were questions about the use of indigenous medicines and ritual technologies, especially in the house of an official of the proselytizing empire, Mónica and

Graça, who anointed their faces, limbs, and breasts with such medicines, left no doubt that their use was widespread.[27]

Now on the offensive, Mónica emphasized that "she, the confessant, does not know any other spells, and that the said black woman, who, as already stated by her, quarreled with her in Mina, and who died in this city, bore this [false testimony] against her because she bore ill will against her." And this was also the case concerning "another manumitted black woman who is in Mina [and] who is called Mesia, with whom Filipe Eanes, who used to be vicar in Mina, had children." That the vicar had children with Mesia, in the context of clerical celibacy, might be scandalous, yet the sexual violence committed by other officials and residents, according to fellow vicar Gonçalo Toscano de Almeida, was commonplace and thus expected. For Mesia, this violence began decades earlier, when she served the residents of São Jorge da Mina; a daughter was recorded in 1519.[28] Mónica, surprisingly, had no children at the time of her trials, whereas Graça had four. Might Mónica have been spared the predatory violence or had it been mitigated through ritual and recourse to indigenous therapeutics? Or did she realize something which Graça had not even though both frequented the villages and their healers?[29]

VIII

Incensed and doubtful, Azambuja told Mónica that "she was manifestly denying the truth," an actuality "which was known and was told by the witnesses, and therefore he admonished her in the name of Our Lord Jesus Christ to fully confess her crimes." Then his anger abated somewhat, and he promised that "if she acted thus and not otherwise, she would be treated mercifully." Mónica did not respond. Instead, she was escorted to her cell in the prison. But the interrogation was not over.[30]

On September 14, over a week later, Mónica was called to appear before the inquisitors in the Holy Inquisition's council chamber to answer additional questions. They asked "whether she was mindful of any other spells she might have cast, above all, whether she called on demons or invoked them." This series of questions proceeded in rapid succession. Inquisitors also wondered "whether she anointed herself with the powders made of redwood with mud so that they [the captain and officials] might love her or that she might become invisible and fly through the air; and whether, after anointing herself [with the powders], she went to gatherings on the back of some demon, to places where they ate, and drank, and reveled, committing any other indecencies." To these absurdities, Mónica responded, "I have never talked with demons or made a pact with them, and *the truth* is that I anointed myself with mud and with powders made of redwood, and with oil and crushed broad bean, which I was taught to make by a black man who was a healer, who lived in a village [Adena] next to the fortress of Mina."[31]

Indeed, Mónica stressed, as if in a closing argument, "I did not anoint myself in order to become invisible, or go to gatherings where one ate and drank, or ride on animals to take me there, or make people love me, but I anointed myself because it was a local custom among the black people and because I saw the other black women and black men do it. And in the basket, as I have said in the above confession, I carried those ointments with which I anointed myself, as well as soap to wash the clothes, and I did not cast any other spells or superstitions, and the local men call those ointments spells." When Mónica stopped speaking, the questions also ceased, and the inquisitors began their deliberations.[32]

In the course of reaching their verdict, the inquisitors returned to an examination of the records delivered from São Jorge da Mina and the confessions of Mónica Fernandes. They then announced a stunning verdict. They were of the "opinion that these were matters of minor importance and unworthy of being remitted to the Ordinary [Justice], [and] ordered that the said Mónica should be taken to the College of the Doctrine of the Faith so that she might be instructed there in matters of faith." The inquisitors, led by Friar Jerónimo de Azambuja, also ordered Mónica "to confess herself and behave like a good Christian, so that she might be released from there." Mónica was then sentenced as a prisoner in the College, to be instructed in Christian orthodoxy, thereby securing a victory for the empire of a certain belief.[33]

IX

The fight for the soul of the empire, or least its driving force, continued but in unexpected ways. In a surprising move, less than two months after her religious incarceration, Mónica was released. But how, and why? Most condemned heretics sentenced to the College of the Doctrine of the Faith spent one to three years in that facility. Yet, on November 3, 1556, the inquisitors Dr. Ambrósio Campelo and Father Master Friar Jerónimo de Azambuja assembled in the council chamber of the Tribunal of the Holy Office in Lisbon. There, they read a petition and then "ordered that the said Mónica Fernandes, mentioned in this petition, should be sent to their presence." When she arrived, "they told her that they were having her released, in view of what she already knew about doctrine." Such a reversal of their verdict was rare and even more so because of the reputation of brutality with which Azambuja prosecuted confessants.[34]

And yet the inquisitors appealed to Mónica, before parting ways, "that she should mind henceforward to go to the College of the Doctrine of the Faith on Sundays and holy days until she fully learned the Christian doctrine; and that she should confess herself on the three Easters of the year, and take the Holy Sacrament whenever her confessor should find fit, and do all the other acts of a good Christian." Mónica was warned, "Never return to Mina again nor leave the Kingdom without permission, and always communicate with people who are virtuous and good Christians." Graça, too, could not return home. And so, exiled without the possibility of parole or of visiting kinfolk and all the villages near the fortress-city, Mónica's victory over the inquisitional empire was partial, not absolute. Naturally, Mónica offered the inquisitors some assurance. She replied, "I will do thus, since I will lodge in the house of Bartolomeu Gonçalves, near Porta Nova [do Mar]," facing the Tagus River and, beyond, the Atlantic Ocean. To Mónica, the river and ocean were disrupters, not bridges, paths of exile and kinlessness, not of homecoming and family. Even so, she was not completely alone as she had brought a niece with her, and together they made their way through uncertainty and displacement.[35]

How did Mónica come to escape the prison and her doctrinal sentence? She persuaded the head of the College of the Doctrine of the Faith, Francisco de São Miguel, to examine her to "see what she knows about the said doctrine, of which she knows (as far as her [knowledge of the] language enables her) how to cross herself, and the Pater Noster, and the Ave Maria, and the Creed." It was São Miguel's belief that, while at the College, Mónica had absorbed enough of the "doctrine that is taught there," "which she learned with great difficulty since her [knowledge of the] language is poor, and for this reason she is not able to learn more of the doctrine than what she knows already." On this basis, he implored Azambuja and his colleagues "to have mercy on her, given that she has spent some of the little money she brought on herself and on a niece brought with her to serve her." In the petition, crafted by São Miguel, he reasoned, "Now she has no more [money] to spend or anyone to give it to her because she is in prison and a foreigner and has no one to help her meet her needs. She requests that she be released, and she will always pray to God for Your Graces' life and prosperity." Whatever our evaluation of Mónica or her spiritual culture and practices, her release represented at least a partial victory against the empire. The certificate issued by São Miguel and her departure from prison on the same day authenticated her truth.

3

"CALLED
BY THEIR HEATHEN NAMES"

Ɔkete ne ketebɔ sɛ din na wɔnsɛ honam.

The lizard and the antelope have similar names, but their appearance is
not the same.

Abusua te sɛ nhwiren, egugu akuo-akuo.

Family names are like flowers; they blossom in clusters.[1]

ONE COULD FIND ADWOA moving between the European medieval fortress planted on her people's soil and the home-grown townships, adjacent to the rocky peninsula on which the fort stood. The foreigners called this edifice São Jorge da Mina. The townspeople called it the large stone building, *abankɛsɛ*. In a universe inhabited by people and places, the fortress and the towns close to it—Adena and Fetu—could easily have been two planets, separate in orbit, yet on a collision course. Her world and soil were golden, an allure so desirable that the Portuguese who called São Jorge their *cidade* were forced to confront the other intruders in ships, armed with cannons and greed, and the noncompliance of her peoples—whom the strangers deluded themselves in believing their vassals. The Portuguese were too small in number and out of necessity relied on the cooperation of her and her people. Cooperation was situational. The foreigners hoped the burden of baptism, a crude proxy for conversion and allegiance, would generate support for, even protection of, their interests. Cooperation worked when it pleased various parties, but it rarely did so. Portugal needed cloth and metals, which they did not produce, and appealed to African tastes, but these changed with the seasons and in the moment. In exchange, Portuguese merchants received gold, but inland suppliers would only come to transact at São Jorge when the roads were unobstructed. Traversing friendly or hostile communities required peace or a truce, agreed to by sometimes impetuous local rulers. Then there were the highway thugs who robbed travelers and traders on the key roads between the forested interior and the coast.

Why did Africans tolerate the strangers? How did Portugal for exactly a century sustain a European monopoly in gold taken from Adwoa's homeland? What was at stake for both was global empire; the elimination of competition on the vast, uncontrollable high seas; international commerce; wealth; and power derived from lands and peoples outside Europe. And on Adwoa's geographically modest but geopolitically crucial patch of earth, all European seekers of global empire, trade, and power— Portuguese (and Spanish after 1580), Dutch, English, French, etc.—fought over her soil, her soul, and her flesh. They sought, in other words, to exploit the gold from her earth, to convert her soul, and to transform her flesh into a chattel. Their attempt would be frustrated, however. And whatever successes were achieved, these were tempered because Adwoa and her people had other intentions in mind.

I

From the first half of the sixteenth century, when gold from Africa propped up Portugal and its nascent empire, the strangers' presence there hinged on the relative acquiescence of Africans in the beliefs of the Portuguese, no matter how shallow or short-lived. This was because none of the other Portuguese sites where African gold was mined surpassed Mina. And while the fortress-city of São Jorge da Mina was Portugal's principal coastal base in Atlantic Africa, the anchor for that vessel was the village-turned-town of Adena. Strangers called it an *aldeia*. When Captain Afonso de Albuquerque maltreated the people of Adena, and they threatened to abandon their settlement, King João III scolded Albuquerque and advised that he defend and sustain his relationship with Adena's population. Otherwise, Portugal would lose them and their services. João III had learned this: Albuquerque treated the leading men of Adena harshly, leaving the settlement depopulated and causing the men who dealt with the inland gold suppliers to move elsewhere. Albuquerque's actions, the king reasoned, stood in opposition to Portugal's interests and to São Jorge da Mina's welfare and its trade. "Since they are Christians and have received the water of baptism," the king explained, "they must be defended, protected and instructed, and not banished." Though João III claimed Adena as his vassal territory, and which offered obedience to the Portuguese, Adena was thousands of miles away from Lisbon, and both he and Albuquerque knew its inhabitants were anything but subservient. Adwoa's free movement between Adena and the fortress-city, paying lip service to the strangers' theology, called attention to how little control Portuguese captains or residents exercised in her forested lands of gold.[2]

At stake, then, was safeguarding a relationship with Adena—and key neighbors like Fetu and the Eguafoɔ—for the town remained the most vital lifeline to the gold that came from the interior to the coast. No doubt the Portuguese king, as well as his subjects, realized who needed whom in that relationship. João III reminded Albuquerque that Adena's people collected and conveyed the wood for all Portuguese ships by means of their seagoing vessels or canoes, purchased goods on a large scale from the same vessels along the coast, and sold them, thereby extending the market for foreign commodities and generating a local appetite for them. João III needed assurances that Albuquerque would not banish Adena residents considered troublesome. The king was stern: "from expelling them, two dangers may result, deaths and robberies." To avoid this, he commanded his captain to have those deserving of punishment pay a fine to the fortress church, or something similar. Adena's leadership used Portuguese protection to become independent of their Akan overlords—Fetu and the Eguafoɔ—but to remain so necessitated that they forfeit partial sovereignty to Portuguese officials at São Jorge da Mina.

Protecting the townspeople and treating them well became official Portuguese policy "because this is in the interests of our fortress there," said the king; "otherwise, besides losing them and the service which we receive from them, the merchants will not come." If Adena was a crucial adhesive that connected strangers to the land, the African merchants were an even more important link, because they negotiated for the gold sourced inland and then brought it to the coast. These merchants also conveyed captives, used as porters or bargaining chips. João III and his successors understood there were wealthy men in Adena, benefiting from both the inland and overseas trade, and that enslaved peoples could be procured from them. But these benefits, underwritten by tactical relationships, dissolved without the voluntary participation of Adwoa and her people, for João III also vitally grasped that gold merchants did not come to Adena and thus the fortress-city "when the land is without them."[3] Portuguese commercial overtures, accented by Christian baptism and names, assumed that the more they persuaded indigenes to hand over their gold and accept the strangers' trade goods and theology, the more their presence in Africa would be worth the price of high mortality in the tropics.

II

Fully visible and human in her own world, Adwoa exists in the Portuguese records only as a name. Although she shared a background with Madu, who was baptized Catarina, neither her voice nor her world was recorded—or at least has survived. Bereft as she was of the kind of trial records we have for Graça and Mónica, and left with a name etched only in passing, we might call the task of telling her story daunting, if not impossible. Though it is tempting, there is no need to fabulate or invent false tales, believing this approach will rescue her from invisibility, or to empower "the" archive with unearned authority over what can be known about her life. Archives of all sorts store, catalog, and curate the extant form of what was recorded. They, like us, have no more power over the records in their holdings; we must then dig deep and wide in countless repositories, rather than rely on the omnipresent archive. The archive is no bogeyman of research, nor a Wizard of Oz, controlling how and if we return to that foreign country called the past. Human history boils down to human action. That her name was Adwoa and that a Portuguese official, likely the chief *alcaide*, recorded it in 1572 owes as much to her and her community's noncompliant action. A transgressor of orthodoxy, she co-authored a place in the historical record.[4]

Through writing, art, and music, the recorders of human lives determine who and what gets chronicled. How their production endures is circumstantial, out of the control of institutional archives and, at times, of the creators themselves. The royal Portuguese archive, the Torre do Tombo ("the tower of the tome"), met its demise in the earthquake and fire that eviscerated more than half of Lisbon in 1755 and, with that catastrophe, whatever else we could have learned about Adwoa. Her birth name (rendered *Aduá*) is instructive because it alerts us to diverse archives. Packaged in this kernel are cultural cues and data that, when mined by an archival sleuth rather than a fiction writer, bring her life at a crucial global moment into clearer view—with gaps and the unknowable included. That the Portuguese official who recorded her name also wrote perhaps the most extensive report about her world, a wide-angled portrait made in the harvest season of 1572, gives us a foundation on which we can build with informed speculation. No doubt of high rank, the official wrote directly to the eighteen-year-old Portuguese king, Sebastião I, boldly outlining a master plan for the colonization of Adwoa's homeland. In four major arguments, he laid out the benefits of colonization, underlined by the success of Brazil, on the basis of what he saw and knew, the world Adwoa freely inhabited and lived in. Rather than invent or falsely believe, we can infer her thinking and feelings—inhabiting the intimate parts of her life—by building upon what is to be found in European-supplied records and in her own cultural archives. Her name will be our entry to, and she will be our guide through, this early-modern world.[5]

III

Adwoa's name was not an exceptional teaser, plucked from the records. Akan names have long been etched into the Portuguese annals, underscoring a subtle yet remarkable feat of agency for those with whom the Portuguese came into contact. If the Portuguese had had things their way, a trail of imposed baptismal names would have bled through the archival stacks of parchment. Instead, from the late fifteenth century onward, we find a whole slew of African names, including an African trader named Akyi, rulers of Fetu called Sakyi and Ahene (lit. "male ruler"), high-ranking representatives named Akwao and Atta Kwao, Akan officials named Akyeampɔn, and the son and brother of an Akan ruler named Atta Kwame and Nipa (lit. "person, human") respectively. Then there was Captain Asa (lit. "to fight" or "war"). Captain Asa lived up to his name or moniker: the Portuguese dreaded "the great wars waged by a black man whose name is Captain Asa, who has raised himself from nothing and become a thief and a highwayman, so that everyone is afraid of him and pays him a tribute. This Asa brings with him three hundred armed men, who are very brave; he does much harm throughout this land, and because of it no merchants come to this [fortress-city] from anywhere." Portuguese liaisons with African male merchants, sovereigns, and sons of rulers guarantee the stubborn presence in the archives of these Akan male names, but free trade among Akan societies also explains the presence of African female traders like Briolanja, who was no anomaly. Yet, rarely were African girls and women tagged in the Portuguese records with their African names. Adwoa, because of her naming, thus takes on added importance.[6]

Although she left little in the strangers' archives, the name Adwoa tells us everything we need to know about her personhood. Mónica Fernandes's and Graça's mobility, shuttling between the fortress-city and neighboring villages, made them known quantities. Adwoa knew about Mónica, deducing she was born before Mónica's exile and trial in Lisbon, and perhaps she also knew something about Graça, the earliest woman from her world to be dispatched to the Portuguese Inquisition. If Mónica and Graça function as starting points to a life, Adwoa would have matched if not exceeded Graça's age, her life stretching from the mid-sixteenth to the first decades of the next century.

Around 1600, a Dutch trader wrote of Adwoa's people, "They give the child a name upon which they have agreed and swear upon it." The interlude between marriage and children was pregnancy, wherein for three months the men "do not sleep with these wives or make love to them." Adwoa's parents would have been wedded, for a child's birth fully consummated marriage. And there is nothing in the records hinting that she or her parents were ostensibly "mulatto" or residents of the fortress-city of São Jorge da Mina. The village of Adena, then, served as her birthplace. There, Adwoa's mother spent the last month of pregnancy, then delivered Adwoa in her house, where men were disallowed, including Adwoa's father. When Adwoa's mother was six or seven months pregnant, a ritual invoking her father's patrilineal lineage called *ntorɔ*—symbolized by semen—provided the father with a place. Underscoring the inborn spiritual bond between father and child was the ritual's aim, since the connection between mother and child—through the corresponding matrilineal principle called *abusua*, itself embodied by blood—was established at conception and nurtured thereafter. Admixtures of semen and blood, ancestry and lineages, formed a mortal out of convergences. And, yet, she needed to be named to register as a new member of these conjoined families.[7]

Adwoa's successful entrance into the world constituted evidence of her father's ntorɔ, for her people held that it protected the developing fetus. Her mother accomplished the same in observing the rituals and taboos of her husband's ntorɔ—for Adwoa's benefit. "As soon as a mother gives birth to a child," onlookers noticed, "the father calls all his neighbors together; they lay the child on the leaf of a tree (for they have no cushions) and drink over the child's body, so that the wine drips on it." Another observer confirmed, "On that day the father gives as large a feast as he can afford." Called *adintoɔ*, this naming ceremony enacted the Monday following Adwoa's birthday highlighted how her people "name their children after the days."[8]

Once born, Adwoa waited her first seven days to receive what a French observer called "customary names." He went on to say, "As soon as the [ɔkɔmfoɔ, healer], or priest, has blessed the child ... the next thing is to give it a name. If the family be above the common rank, the infant has three names given it; the first is the name of the day of the week on which it is born; the next, if a son, is the grandfather's name, and if a girl, the grandmother's; others give their own name, or that of fame of their relations." And so there appeared Amma, Akua, Akosua, Afia, and Adwoa. These were common day-names called *kradin*, a complementary set of male–female names. Added to them were some European names, but this was "practiced only by those that live under the protection of the forts on the coast." The presence of European-Christian names offered no surprises; Graça and Mónica used baptismal names when they were recorded as speaking. The Frenchman's qualification, however, held true for many who existed outside the fortified walls as well as outside the reach of Portugal's authority.[9]

Amid the girls and women named Akua, Afia, and Yaa, Adwoa stood out as a Monday-born child, which is to say her soul came to the earth on a Monday.[10] Mothers and fathers, husbands and wives had their own dwellings, and so whereas Adwoa was born in her mother's house, her adintoɔ occurred at her father's house. Waiting seven days ensured she remained on earth and did not prematurely return to *asamandoɔ*, the abode of her spiritual mother. Until the week after her birth, Adwoa was a stranger greeted with hopes of her staying and wishes for her long life. Naming, as the onlookers suggest, remained the responsibility of the father's family. Apparently, Adwoa was born on one of six Mondays on the Akan calendar of 378 days, subdivided into nine periods of 42 days. Each period, called *adaduanan*, was again subdivided into six weeks of seven days. The root of Adwoa's name—*dwo*—performed a specific role, for it plotted out the spiritual force associated with the Monday-born, known as *Adwo*. Viewed as an extension of a cosmic force, this spiritual force, this *ɔbosom*, formed a bond with Adwoa at birth. A Protestant Dutchman wrote dismissively, "Each particular person hath his peculiar false God, which he or she worships ... on that day of the week in which he was born. This they call their *bossum*." Monday-born persons often shared similar qualities and personal challenges, and Adwoa was characteristically calm, peaceful, and agile, a protector and supplicant who avoided conflicts and yet had a confidence that made her unreceptive to external advice.[11]

Through the optic of Adwoa's name, her character is revealed. A Danish clergyman wrote of Adwoa's people that they "celebrate every week the day on which they are born." Fortuitously, his celebratory illustration targeted the Monday-born. He tells us, "[Take], for instance, Monday. On that day in the morning before washing themselves, they grind up [a plant] in water and take a mouthful of the water three times, and every time they spit out the water they pray to [Onyankopɔn]," one of a multitude of praise names accenting the qualities of a cosmic force.[12] For Adwoa, the Monday-born with a cool and peaceful character tempered with bouts of ingratitude, morning rituals such as these affirmed her connection to that cosmic force, parceled out into her spiritual force or Adwo. Adwoa would have been taught these and other rituals, a pattern set in motion by a naming ritual that advised her to seek and tell the truth and to distinguish it from falsehood, as she strove for an ethical, even ideal, life called *abrabɔ*.[13]

Adwoa was also guaranteed a second, family name called *agyadin*, originating from her father's patrilineal clan. Each patrilineal clan possessed its own day of observance when members ritually cleansed their souls near a body of water, exchanged greetings with specific responses among those sharing the same ntorɔ, upheld a set of taboos, respected a sacred animal which members tabooed, shared basic character qualities, and assumed one of several agyadin. There is no way of knowing Adwoa's agyadin or ntorɔ, but, if we speculate further, she may have been associated with the Bosomnkɛteaa/Bosompo ntorɔ, for it was linked to the ocean near which she and her family lived and where she would have purified her soul. The veracity of Adwoa's ties to this composite ntorɔ is not the object of this reasoned exercise in probability. In this world of probability, Adwoa would have responded to members of this ntorɔ group with *Yaa anyaado* or *opeafo* and learned to cleanse her soul on Tuesdays by the ocean. She would have avoided dogs, doves, and tortoises on Tuesdays, but regarded the hippopotamus, appropriately called a sea horse, as sacred and not to be harmed or killed. This Adwoa would have been socialized to be proud and audacious—the basic character of the Bosomnkɛteaa/Bosompo ntorɔ—and given an agyadin such as Dakwa, Boadu, Bonsu, Kusi, Poakwa, Otutu, Ayimadu, or

Okurofa. Let us call her, for the sake of this exercise, Adwoa Bonsu. Bonsu, meaning whale or another sea animal spouting water, seems fitting and within the limits of plausibility.[14]

IV

A Catholic cleric and editor of a global atlas project, *Civitates Orbis Terrarum* (cities of the world), published in 1572 a bird's-eye view of Adwoa's village of Adena and the São Jorge da Mina fortress. Anchored some miles out to sea are three Portuguese caravels, alongside one of which is a canoe with two rowers and a coxswain. Facing the ocean, in front of the fortress, lies a small chapel dedicated to São Jorge (Saint George), adjacent to three rows of thatch-roofed structures. To the left of the fortress is a bridge to the village of Adena. A mixture of two large houses and numerous smaller conical abodes dot the rectangular perimeter of the village. Neighboring the village is a chapel, smaller than the São Jorge one, while opposite the fortress, across the Benya lagoon and the river that snakes behind it, stands a small chapel on a hill dedicated to São Jago (Saint James). Still further behind Adena, somewhere in the hinterlands, are the territories of three kings. In the editor's Latin addendum, he mentioned the king of Portugal who had ordered the building of the fortress in 1482, and adverted to the gold exchanged by African merchants for textiles and other articles of trade. The need for locally sourced gold and the desire for foreign things made Adwoa's Adena a crossroads between dueling forces—indigenous and Catholic, African and European, source and destination of gold and goods.

Adena was located where the lagoon formed from an interior river, bisecting the settlement before pouring into the Atlantic Ocean. This was a place that faced the ocean, the fortress, the hinterland polities of the Eguafoɔ and Fetu, and their respective coastal villages of Akatakyi and Cape Corso (Oguaa). "In the old days," explained a Dutch cartographer who consulted local experts, the Eguafoɔ, Fetu, and Asebu "used to be under one king." He continued, "But they are now divided into those three, who live on the coast." Could they be the three kings? The Eguafoɔ had built a vast inland town with a large population of fishers, farmers, and traders. Interior towns were larger, more populous and powerful, and richer in gold than coastal towns and villages. Akatakyi remained the Eguafoɔ's principal coastal village, while Fetu's was Oguaa. Fetu's peoples procured fish from Oguaa in exchange for foodstuffs and gold. Oguaa and the Eguafoɔ fed Adena with fish and foodstuff, respectively. In a time before Europeans, half of Adena was under the Eguafoɔ and the other under Fetu, "who came there to collect their contribution, but that subjection has been annulled a few years ago by some Portuguese Governor, so that they live now as a republic on their own and are mostly governed by the Portuguese Governor." Skilled as fishers, canoe builders and rowers, and bead polishers, Adena villagers were at best situational Christians in that liminal space, neither independent nor fully subjugated. Adwoa would have been elderly by the time Adena became this semi-subjugated polity, linked to nominal Portuguese authority. Hers was a time without kings for Adena, and it does not seem it ever had one.[15]

Adwoa was familiar with the three subdivisions of the village, each with its own head. Their streets were irregular and narrow, coiling around the buildings and houses, some built with masonry but all packed together in partitioned compounds of three or four linked dwellings. In these square or rectangular compounds, many people lived together, each family with its own abode. One observer wrote, "The walls are interlaced with wattle and daubed with earth. The roof is made of palm fronds." Holes in the walls for fresh air and sunlight took the place of windows. Inside the houses, the observer continued, "the walls are coated with red earth; the floor too is red, like red ochre." In the middle of the many bedrooms and alcoves remained an open space for cooking, washing, and housework. "This space which is square," another onlooker tells us, "is kept particularly clean and tidy, since every day the bondswomen must smear it with white or red earth, which they consider a particularly beautiful way of decorating the house." Of equal aesthetic value were the hairstyles Adwoa and her people wore: "black people wear their hair in many different ways, one of them with so many knots and tangles, in which they put gold beads, and others which they buy, and reels like those for linen, and loops and slipknots." The observer concluded that these stylings represented "sensuality and brazenness."[16]

The elongated village was prone to floods, situated as it was by the lagoon and ocean, and so villagers erected stone walls and ditches to protect their structures and lifeways. The families inhabiting the village formed a community of fishers, traders, interpreters, and captive peoples, as well as so-called mulattos and some baptized individuals whom Europeans collectively called idolatrous half-Christians. Regardless of these distinctions, old age, memory, and culture transmission were highly regarded. "So no one is promoted to a rank of honor," wrote yet another observer, "until he has reached a considerable age." And among the aged, revered by outsiders for their powerful and accurate memory, "They strengthen their memories by zealously repeating the old stories ... Young people and children listen to such discourse with avid ears, and absorb it in their hearts. In this way, knowledge of past matters is always propagated." Besides her baptismal name of Maria, it is difficult to tell the precise place Adwoa held in this community. And, yet, her village held enough importance for it to be colonized, along with the wider region, by the Portuguese empire. Adwoa was without doubt a witness to it all.[17]

V

It was a time of flux in the empire, and at last its teenage sovereign agreed to a century-long push for free trade. In the 1570s the Crown abandoned its trade monopoly over Mina; instead, this commerce was handed over to a consortium of merchants. Merchants, members of the king's council, and ordinary functionaries felt that this moment was an opening, an opportunity to seize. And, so, numerous proposals came before the king. The unnamed official who recorded Adwoa's name was one of these petitioners. His advantage, perhaps greater than that of others, stemmed from his experience and his current view of Adwoa's homeland in real time, unlike politicians and merchants in Lisbon who had never set foot on African soil. He put forward four strategies to maximize the benefits of Mina, short-hand for the fortress-city and the entire coast. First, leave matters as they were, provided some reforms took place. Second, implement changes to increase profit for the Crown at lower costs. Third, lease the Mina trade, though this he considered a non-starter, undeserving of further consideration. Finally, expand commerce through colonization, whereby Mina would be populated by Portuguese nationals, "which is what I think," reasoned the official, "most befits the service of God and of Our Lord the King." Adwoa and her people, not to mention their land, had no articulated position in these designs, except as subjects of empire—or, at least, so the sponsors of empire believed.

The galleys concerned the Portuguese the most. Their protection from interlopers and their trade position remained tenuous. Galleys were low, flat ships propelled mainly by rowing but with one or more sails, in case of favorable winds. Used principally for warfare and trade, they were manned by Portuguese convicts whose commuted sentences required that they be stationed on the margins of the empire. The further away from Lisbon—for convicts also circulated within Portugal—the more severe the crime and punishment. The official argued, "No white prisoners should be put on the galleys." He had his reasons. First, "they are not good for work in this land, and a black man rowing is worth two of them." Secondly, the infirmary bore great expense because the white prisoners were often sick. Third, and "incomparably worse," many of these Portuguese convicts, from thieves to those sentenced to death, "live unlawfully with native black women, who, as has been ascertained, waste births, whether killing them after they are born or provoking miscarriages." What this implied was abortion or, worse, murder. It implicated women like Adwoa, and proof of their alleged crime rested on an observation: "There is not one mulatto in the whole village, whereas there are many in those places where black women give birth safely."[18]

If there was sexual violence, surely Portuguese convicts, residents, and officials were not blameless. Indeed, the perpetrators of sexual violence against girls and women of Adwoa's village and homeland ranged from the fortress governor to those subject to his authority. Adwoa lived through the governorship of João Rodrigues Pessanha, who was known as a sexual predator and was tried by the Inquisition in 1588 for "sins of the flesh, with both Christian and Heathen women." Twenty-three witnesses testified against him, including men who worked with him and under his command. Several specified that in Pessanha's house "he kept black women, with whom he sinned." More telling is that "he had his black men bring him by force the daughters or nieces of black women, so as to sleep with them." Rape was routine for women and girls, for he "opened the girls with his hands, when he could not do it otherwise." One witness explained, "He had his black men take the black women because they did not want to live with him as mistresses, and so he slept with them forcibly; and I say this because his black men told me so, shocked as they were by seeing him behaving thus." But who were these African men? Pessanha "had his slaves take daughters by force from their parents, and under threat and menace the said parents gave them to the slaves," clarified another witness. The assistance his captives provided was specified: "His slaves held them by their legs and arms when they did not comply in any other way."[19]

Several witnesses indicated that the girls and women so violated came from Fetu and Adena, and that Pessanha even supported and gave presents to some, calling them around midday to his dwelling. Could Adwoa have been one of those women? Eerily plausible, of course, because Pessanha was no anomaly or rare predator. Indeed, his ritual acts of repetitive violence were, in the words of a witness, "customary among men in this fortress." One witness, a forty-year-old soldier, knew some of these African women but did not mention their names for the record. Other women among the nameless included hostages from Winneba and the Eguafoɔ, "who were taken to his house, and he locked himself with them." The elderly Pessanha offered a plea to the Inquisition, characterizing himself as a "sensual sinner, endeavoring to satisfy my savage appetite and nothing more." Admittedly, he continued, "I have defiled those black women who were virgins with my hand, because age would not permit me to do so anymore." Then came the telling remark: "And if there is any excuse in this, it lies in my being misled by their all bearing Christian names, and this is so widespread in those parts that it is not condemned by confessors any more than other sensual sin with a Christian woman outside matrimony." The seventy-four-year-old Pessanha pleaded with the inquisitors for mercy and absolution of his crimes and sins. He was sentenced to four months in a monastery, being required to pay the case expenses and to confess each month. Nothing about African girls and women or sexual violence found its way into the General Council of the Holy Inquisition's decision. And, two days after his sentencing, Pessanha received a pardon in the name of King Philip I.[20]

Sexual predation was only one form of imperial violence; labor was another. The galleys needed crews and rowers, who were recruited from captive and free African boys and men. Rather than use white rowers serving out their punishment, the official endorsed the idea of sentencing "the black criminals of São Tomé and of the island of Fogo [belonging to Cape Verde] to the galleys, whether for a certain period of time or for good, according to the nature of the crime." And all the captured "foreign privateers and the Lutherans [Dutch] who come to make raids, if they are not hanged straight away, should be put to the oars until they die, with no more courtesy than is used with black people." Naturally, the official contended, "black men, who will better endure continuous work," would handle and transport ivory for gold, protect the land, and capture pirates. The galleys, then, served as a labor-intensive means to deter competitors inasmuch as they facilitated trade and helped patrol the coast and provision it with foreign goods, involving "little communication with the black people." And, yet, interaction with Adwoa's people was necessary, not an option. The official, perhaps grasping his blunder, stressed the need to address them, but with a "conversation with these black men to make them understand that, as long as they remain good and faithful vassals of Our Lord the King, His Highness will take care of them and protect them as subjects, but not in such a way they might imagine being friends with Our Lord the King." There was a fear that indigenes might reject a subjugated and laboring position, that they might consider their own rulers on a par with rulers in Europe. The official tells us there was a "black man whom they call King of the Forest," the whole of which was three times the size of Portugal. For colonization to work, the judicial powers of local leaders had to be usurped, and "not one of them be in any way given the title of King," for "when one of these black men calls himself, or wants to be called, King, he fancies that being King of the Eguafoɔ or Fetu ... is the same as being King of Portugal." How dare they![21]

Subjugation, if it were to happen, would require assent to Portugal's theology. Having been baptized and assigned the name Maria, Adwoa might have intuited the extent of colonial claims to her homeland and peoples—renting land on which to retain a fortified presence, but pursuing another kind of conquest through baptism, chapel attendance, doctrine classes, bribery, and the symbolic power and prestige assumed from quasi-membership in the foreigner's empire. Vicars of the fortress-city worked to persuade indigenes to attend Mass and doctrine classes, both in the fortress and in Adena. Newly arrived priests did likewise, "each of them in his own place teaching doctrine and reading," explained the official, who claimed, "I saw many black people, boys and young men, with sheets of paper and books in their hands." Whatever optimism was raised by seeing these potential converts, the official was quick to charge, "Among these Christian black people there is much filthiness—which could be called something much worse—because Christian men marry heathen women, and Christian women heathen men, according to their heathen uses, and none of them is married as Holy Mother Church commands." The official pondered the reality, not his hope, and reasoned, "in order that these black people become better Christians, they should live together in the area closest to the fortress, given that it is very prejudicial for a Christian to be among twenty heathens, where I think they all live as heathens, and cast their *feitiços*, and make use of superstitions and indecency." This charge cast a wide net over people like Adwoa and those who were not baptized. A friar who lived among Adwoa and her people shared the same sentiment.[22]

VI

Peering through the half-open door of potential colonization, by means of theology and trade, the official could see building more fortresses remained essential work. Another fortress, then the next, was crucial to forming a network of fortified bases, integral to creating allied communities seduced by the stranger's dogma, that would baptize more like Adwoa but keep her and others fixated on being Maria, on being a colonial subject. Their fate, if colonization was to succeed, was that of renters subjugated and living on their own lands. "I believe it will be most advantageous to have a fortress built," wrote the official to the king, "but next to some salt pans which are very close by, and to have the salt pans repaired by slave workers under the command of white men." If Adwoa's homeland was to be populated under a colonial scheme, she and her people would be forbidden to make "salt through boiling sea water, which is how they presently do it." A German eyewitness detailed that her people subsisted principally on agriculture, fishing, hunting, trading, livestock husbandry, and various crafts, but among these salt making was a major industry in itself. "Not only is this salt sold daily in the market by black women," he wrote, "but large quantities are also carried a great distance inland in special baskets for sale." Adwoa's living or working in a major salt-producing village suggests that she had a role in the salt trade as well as a voice in rejecting colonial designs to undermine it.[23]

The overriding desire for gold persisted alongside dealings in ivory, beads, foreign textiles, and locally produced cotton cloths, which the Portuguese called *bandas*, made of "two strips of cotton one or two palms wide that the native and white people buy." Adwoa and her peoples used this striped cloth, called Mandinga cloth, for garments and covering themselves, while "the white people [buy and] sell [it] when the occasion arises."

Transactions such as these required a medium of exchange, a currency, but the official complained that "no kind of currency is used" and advised the king "to create some currency, which would circulate only here, and order that it be used by both white and black men and be accepted without exception." Gold dust and weights and iron-stone currencies were used in trade among indigenes, but these were distinct from Portuguese coinage, defying easy comparison and recognition. Adwoa would have known and used these currencies, especially in acquiring a range of imported products: linen for beds and tables, tableware, basins, chamber pots, blankets, cups, woolen and cotton cloths, old clothes, wax candles, coral, soap, barrels of flour, preserves; and for herself, women's shirts, black dresses, knee-high boots, shoes, and headdresses. Also imported from neighboring lands, but found and used locally as a spice and medicinal accompaniment, melegueta peppers or grains of paradise (*Aframomum melegueta*) formed a spice trade from West Africa, rivaling but never outdoing the gold trade.[24]

Gold lured the Portuguese to Adwoa's homeland and kept them there. They had been present there for a century when the official recorded Adwoa's name, and throughout that time enquiries and searches for new gold mines went on uninterruptedly. The proposal for colonization stuck to this old tune, and for good reason. "Should there be mines—as there are—[we need] to build," insisted the official, "as soon as a mine is found, a fortress, or an ample house for white people." For Adwoa and her people, an assemblage of rocks forming a small fortification would suffice, close to the white people's house, next to which "huts could be made for the black people working [there]." Absolutely convinced Adwoa's land had more gold, the official believed workers would mine it there, for "almost everywhere that the black people are said to have searched for it, they have found it." Still, Adwoa's people "do not open mines or search for gold in places which are not close to the water that is used to separate it from the soil. And even if they find it elsewhere, they do not dig there because of the labor of taking the soil to where there is water." The Portuguese would solve this challenge of water and distance by digging "wells, or aqueducts, wherever there are conditions for bringing water from the rivers, or else they will take the soil on beasts of burden, which they will raise, or on the black people themselves, who of all things are best at carrying." The comparison of her people to beasts of burden would not have been lost on Adwoa, especially if she or her kinfolk were porters, routinely subjected to carrying head-loads of foreign goods from the coast into the densely forested interior.[25] Captives and porters put to work—either exploiting mines or conveying merchandise—were the consequences, and not the cause, of the gold trade. If gold enticed the strangers' initial visits, after a century Adwoa's land held a bounty that triggered visions of permanent settlement.[26]

VII

Inside the forested land something rustled. The taste of gold filled the strangers, but the bounty of the land prepared them and Adwoa's people for more. The Portuguese had introduced new cultigens, crops from the Americas such as maize, adding to an already remarkable variety of starches, most notably staple yams. "I also think that it is not senseless for there to be others, besides the black people who will dig in the mines, to break the soil together with them and plant corn and yams," declared the official, "and for them to bring palm wine and nuts, and anything else which could provide for their subsistence and for that of those who dig." Others might procure and then breed livestock for the Portuguese, who would need less if any supplies were dispatched from Portugal beyond wheat flour and wine. But

Adwoa's fertile ground provided much food for consumption. Palm oil replaced olive oil, maize did the same for the Portuguese staple wheat bread, and *bordão* wine harvested year-round at Akyem, near the Manso ("Ankobra") river, surpassed the Portuguese variety. Yet, palm wine remained a year-round option that lasted longer than *bordão* wine. The official hoped, by making these adjustments, that imperial expenditures would drop and profits increase, for "there would be no need in the Kingdom to be concerned about supplies."[27]

In the village, Adwoa and community members consumed lots of fish but very few cattle. Added to these were ample yields of millet, yam, honey, water, and palm wine. Theirs was a pescatarian diet. Looking out from the fortress and onto Adwoa's land, the official marveled. "There are oranges, lemons, and citrons, and sugarcane, meadows of green amaranth, much purslane, and a kind of eggplant which is very good to eat," he reported. The peppers resembled those from the Caribbean; the white and red pumpkins looked like melons. "There are a thousand kinds of fruit good to eat," he continued, "[each] so marvelous that it whets the appetite." Adwoa and "the black people eat them all ... And all of them grow naturally." Instinctively, the official had little doubt about "the seeds which have been brought from Portugal, [for] I have not heard of any that has not grown here. There is radish, cabbage, coriander, and mint, and clove, [and] basil, which I believe grows wild. Every seed grows, and if it does not bear any grain (as happened with a few wheat seeds, which grew as high as a man and with many ears) it seems to me that this is not due to the nature of the soil." Indeed, orange and lemon orchards thrived near the fortress, as well as fig and pomegranate trees and vines from Portugal bearing grapes. In a phrase, "whatever is sown grows."[28]

Adwoa and her fellow villagers planted and harvested a large type of maize which they called *aburo*, the same crop Spaniards in the Caribbean and in Spain called Indian wheat. Maize, millet, and sorghum (guinea corn) are similar, but whereas maize was introduced from the Americas, sorghum and millet were not, for these "they have always had, and they made do with [them] before the Portuguese came," wrote a Dutch interloper. Often the European-supplied records confuse rather than make clear these distinctions, especially between millet and maize. A German observer noticed what Adwoa would have known intuitively, that the "daily food of the natives consists mainly of bread [using a grain the foreigner termed *milie*], which they call *cantje*, and then also vegetables, fruit, and fish." Cantje or *kenkay* is a fermented white corn dish. Of the grain termed *milie*, there were small and large types, the large one maize and the small kind millet. Not only was maize in Adwoa's time a crop commonly grown throughout her region, but markets were filled every day with African women selling millet-and-maize-based products, fresh fish, and fish fried in palm oil, as well as plantains, melegueta peppers, and yams. If wheat bread was the Portuguese staple, indigenous yams were its local counterpart, to which we might add cocoyam and plantains, which were much consumed in Akyem and Adena. When English intruders arrived on Adwoa's shores and traded near her village, they, too, were struck by her people's diet and foods. Their senses were infiltrated by an ensemble of local herbs, fish, beans, peppers, and wheat products, and a bread made of ground maize—"another 'sort' of corne which is called *mill*."[29]

Adwoa's people in Adena obtained sheep, goats, pigs, cows, and calves from Portugal or through Portuguese merchants working in Benin and São Tomé. Some of these, such as pigs, were reared in the fortress-city as early as the 1490s. Our official's knowledge of domestic animals was confined to goats, sheep, and cows. He observed that these were very small. As for other animals, he reported, the "pigs which are brought adapt well here, but not so in Akyem, where the Governor's horses and a donkey died. Dogs adapt to the land." The tsetse fly, transmitter of the parasites (trypanosomes) causing sleeping sickness, inflicted much pain and even death upon cattle, horses, donkeys, and pigs. These flies also infect humans, and Adwoa would have been acutely aware of them and their parasites. Given her diet, she would have had little contact with the multitude of animals thus infected. But this situation faced threats from the colonization scheme. The official envisioned "a certain number of goats, pigs, and sheep brought in the *caravelão* [sent from São Tomé], or in other vessels, and give[n] to the black people in threes." As these animals were useful and inexpensive, Adwoa's people would "keep not less than the number given to them but, on the contrary, more; and let them not kill the females to stop them from repro-ducing; and let them raise herds and have shepherds to take them to the bush during the day and bring them back to the house of their owners at night." The official also pointed to the advantages of the "freshwater rivers [that] enter the sea, where many sugar mills might be built, since there is an infinite quan-tity of timber along their banks." Livestock rearing alongside sugar production, married to an extractive timber industry—for the "variety of trees which provide timber is endless"—foretold profits beyond the red and yellow dyes that indigenes used for cotton cloths and caps. And, naturally, there was "very good cotton in this land, which could be of much profit."[30]

VIII

"Truly, if one would want to write in detail about all the things this land gives, one would never end," wrote the official, in what proved to be his closing argument for colonization. Surely Adwoa and her countrywomen and men would have accepted these details as "proof of the generosity of the land," but would they have accepted their place in the colonial designs for it? This official's report was written in 1572, the same year that Luís Vaz de Camões published his national epic poem, *Os Lusíadas*. The Portuguese are the heroes in the poem, which is dedicated to King Sebastião. Often compared with other European epic tales, Camões's praise poem attended to Portugal's global ascendancy, paying homage to his countrymen in Asia, but saying very little about Africa. Apparently, Adwoa's slice of Africa had no gold, had not funded the empire-to-be, had not provided the strangers with ecologies and cultures other than their own. This was not erasure; it was an implicit concession to an essential irony: whereas Portuguese sea power and tyranny set up nominal control in the Indian Ocean world for their benefit, that did not happen on Adwoa's land. Though both the official and Camões made proposals to Sebastião, for this moment would be the most crucial turning point in the empire's history, colonization may explain why some pushed for the scheme while others pushed it, like Adwoa's Africa, to the side.

The official had no ambiguity about where he and several others stood: "This land should be given to be populated, and could very easily become a new Portugal, or new Indies, richer than those of Castile [Spain], which will be a greater reason for our descendants to be proud." Rather than being counted among those "who missed the opportunity which had been there for so long and would have been so easy to seize," he pleaded, the Portuguese should seize the chance, for inaction would lead the Africans "to defend themselves from us, and [realize] how to expel us from their lands, and not how to be Christians." To avert this eventuality, the case was made for how to proceed with colonization, in spite of the fate that awaited Adwoa and her people.[31]

First, colonization would add new kingdoms to those already possessed by Portugal, "submitting them to its laws and having the divine laws preached." There was a sense regarding Adwoa's people that "they estimate [Portugal] to be inferior to their own [kingdoms], because of the gold which exists there and that they must know to be a better metal than that of the *manillas*" of the Portuguese. Colonization would erase this sentiment. Surely, they should proceed "as was done in the government of India, [namely] that a grand nobleman came to this land as Viceroy of Ethiopia [Africa], as he goes to India and used to go to Brazil, with succession in the government should God dispose of him." The official, fearing this nobleman might not come, given the view of West Africa as the white man's grave, argued that "whatever kills here would also kill in the healthiest part of Spain, namely a scarcity of products from their own country." He then targeted specific behaviors that those who came to Mina should avoid: "going around naked and sleeping on the floor; walking barefoot exposed to the sun and the rain." There were also drawbacks as far as physicians and medicines sent from Portugal were concerned, "because the greater part of the physicians take too long to understand the diseases of the land, and when the medicines do arrive they are so only in name; and in addition to these are bad diets which, by themselves, would be enough to kill people in healthy lands." Colonization could not succeed if the colonists killed themselves in the process.[32]

Adwoa might have made out only the general shape of this argument, but she and her peoples understood how to live on and with the land. They were not immune to the diseases which afflicted indigenes and foreigners; they simply had coded wisdom or built-up knowledge and quasi-immunity. For instance, guinea worm disease caused by a parasite in contaminated drinking water terrorized both parties. There are no initial symptoms until, a year later, painful blisters erupt with the worm emerging from the skin over a few weeks. Adwoa and neighbors used palm oil and plant medicines. "The [Africans] heal themselves," noted one observer, "and when they have pulled the worm out the length of a finger, they cut it off, smear palm oil on it and tie a green leaf on instead of a plaster. Similarly they heal the swelling which forms afterwards by cutting it open and letting the impure matter run out: they wash it with water strongly mixed with pepper and other herbs, so that it stings sharply; afterwards they put palm oil and a leaf on it, to relieve [the pain]. This remedy they use for all their open injuries." This onlooker also commented: "For stomach-ache I have seen them use ground-up herbs mixed with earth [clay] and made wet. With these they cover the body where it hurts, or they quench [iron] in beer or palm wine and drink it, as hot as they can bear it." Indeed, "For smallpox, syphilis, swollen glands, headache, and hot fevers, they heal themselves and need no special people."[33]

It seemed colonization would never be realized, for, after health and leadership concerns, there was the problem of personnel. Portugal was a small country, with an equally small population of just over a million inhabitants. In the time of the colonization plans, noblemen and convicts populated the far reaches of the empire, which was stretched almost to its staffing limits. Critics of colonizing Mina, the official imagined, might have thought "populating this land will be prejudicial to India, because there will not be enough people to go there," and so he "proposed that no people come from Portugal, and that permission only be given to those from all these islands, from São Tomé to the Azores, which, I believe, are overflowing with people." There were apparently people in São Tomé eager to populate Mina: "there were twenty men or more who would come, each of them bringing one hundred of his captive slaves, among whom are many very worthy craftsmen of all the crafts necessary now at the beginning, as builders, masons, blacksmiths, and the like." But as the captains and governors of the forts and settlements were members of the Portuguese nobility, the male and presumably female settlers would thus fall under the jurisdiction of officials who were "native-born Portuguese." The galleys would, then, cruise along the coast, facilitating trade and shielding the soon-to-be-colonized land from Portugal's European enemies.[34]

If something moved on the horizon, it would be all the benefits that colonization brought with it. It is curious that rarely did Africans request vessels as items of trade, and equally uncommon was the European desire to allow local shipbuilding, especially on the African mainland. Colonial benefits, the official argued, required constraints, and the prohibition of shipbuilding was one. He knew he had to say it was unwise to let vessels be built on Adwoa's land. The thought of allowing vessels to sail further than from coast to coast filled him with a desire to appease the king and so this, too, would be controlled, apart from the king's ships or those he allowed. The greater the restrictions, the greater the benefits to the Crown, and populating the land "more rapidly with white Christians [permits ...] their farming, and cattle breeding, and plowing the land, from which they would also reap much benefit."[35]

What benefits might accrue to Adwoa or her people? Proximity. "If the land is populated and the black and the white people live side by side," wrote our official, "I fear that the white people might be bad neighbors to the black people." Yet, "If they lived together in the villages, thus the black people would benefit from human civilization, and learn the methods of cultivating the land and raising stock used by the Portuguese; and they would also benefit from the Christian religion, the children of the black people being raised together with those of the white people and learning the language." Conquest is one thing, but colonization by western Europe is a strange creature, requiring the colonized to erase their cultural hard-drive and reinscribe on it imitated speech, behaviors, and beliefs. There was something else, something sinister and at odds: "when the black people outnumber the white, they can be mixed with each other as seems best." And yet, the same official argued, "it will be necessary to do with these black people the same that is done in Spain with the vagabonds who are made to look for a master and start working, punishing them monetarily and even physically if they do not do so, for they are the most idle and lazy people in the world."[36] To be sure, comparisons were drawn to prove a simple point: "we may call those from the Indies meek and simple lambs, while these [Africans] are wild, wicked wolves." Race and religion, morphed into culture, outmaneuvered other considerations.

Obliterating local ideas and cultural forms through conversion formed a baseline expectation—a person "can always be made useful until they finally convert." Underlying processes of racial mixing and religious conversion, however, was suspicion as well as fear. And, so, the official argued that indigenes should be forbidden to use "any kind of Spanish arms, while ensuring that the white people do not let theirs get rusty; and in order that they be more prepared, they should be ordered to take muster every so many days, and live in such a way among the black people that these, without being hurt, are afraid of them, because no matter how pampered they are by the white people, believe me, they will never be their friends." That Adwoa discarded the name Maria, spent her time among her own people, and paid only lip service to the fog of baptism suggests another assessment of colonization and the benefits implied in it.[37]

IX

It was when the silence fell that the official realized his proposal would remain just that—a proposal among many others sent to a young, misguided sovereign who died in a Moroccan crusade seeking to reclaim a valor of old. Sebastião met his ancestors, the same ones who reached manhood through the spilling of Muslim blood and pillage in North Africa. There, the launching pad for the empire now became its deathbed. It is fitting perhaps that the empire birthed in North African warfare in the early fifteenth century should effectively be no more because of victorious African warfare in the late sixteenth century. Mina, too, achieved a victory of sorts—no colonization, no conquest. Indeed, as Portugal and its empire soon plunged into civil war and were then devoured by Philip II of Spain in 1580, the Portuguese presence in Adwoa's homeland became less secure. The Dutch would oust them, followed by an arms race among no less than six European nations for gold, commodities, and captives on Adwoa's land.

It is not clear if colonization would have worked anyway. There were no centralized polities, as in Brazil and wherever else the Portuguese set up shop, and so they had to contend with multiple, competing polities with large armed forces and with possession of land and its gold. Perhaps Adwoa was watching all this on her treks between the village and the fortress, when the realization dawned that the Portuguese were weak and would be defeated. Little could have been lost on her. She lived in the village, in some ways an adjunct to the fortress but in others a different world. She probably worked in the fortress-city and certainly was known to its Portuguese officials, including the official who wrote the proposal we have described. In the end, it was people like Adwoa who sabotaged Portuguese ideological conquest and its contemplated colonial scheme: few of her people on the coast and further inland practiced the Christian faith, and even the inducement of cash rewards to governors at São Jorge da Mina for each convert did not work, as most converts failed to remain Christians. The killing of all but one of the Augustinian clergy in the 1570s underscores that conquest through

Christianization, with the exception of a handful of baptized African rulers and their sons, was as strong as the Portuguese presence and power on Adwoa's coast.[38]

If Adwoa was a young woman in the 1570s, her elder self in the 1630s may have witnessed the replacement of the strangers with a new cast of European entrants. What endured, even as the fortress-city still stood without its original occupants, was her name and the culture to which it remained tightly braided. Two centuries after her name appeared in the official's proposal, three centuries after the Portuguese established a stronghold on a rocky peninsula in proximity to Adwoa's village, a Danish slave merchant penned these words: "Those Europeans whom the Blacks especially like are known most of the time by black [*sic*] names. It is a common practice that, *when new Europeans arrive in that country they are each given a name during their first eight days*, and it is amusing that *the names they are given are rather well suited to their temperaments and the condition of their bodies*." If power is the ability to define a reality and have others accept that reality as if it were their own, then power, or different kinds of powers, were wielded by indigenes, who preserved and then imposed upon strangers their naming culture. Intruders named as an Akan person could invoke culture and its ideological force but without incorporation into clans and without obligations flowing from membership.

"Names are changed, too," the merchant acknowledged, when European behavior changed.[39] Implied here is an approach to human nature and human development that is situational and cyclical. Change accompanied Adwoa at the precise moment she transitioned. The *mmogya* (blood) forming the physiological bond between Adwoa and her mother, including the formation of flesh and physical body, became a corpse fading into the earth that could not be colonized. Adwoa's soul or *kra*, which had sprouted on a Monday and had sustained her conscience and life, recycled into a cosmic force. Her spirit perished or morphed, and either it or the *mmogya* became an ancestral spirit awaiting rebirth through a woman of the same *abusua*. Through libations and rituals of remembrance, and the newborn, Adwoa's name prevailed even if it did not achieve a modicum of immortality.

EPILOGUE

Nkrabea nni kwatibea.

There are no means of avoiding destiny.

Mmosea twa wo nan ase a, ɛfiri fie.

If a pebble cuts the bottom of your foot, it is from your own home.

WE ALL KNOW SOMETHING of the power of ideas, and the stories that convey them. The stories of the three women narrated in this book—Graça, Mónica, and Adwoa—featured a set of cultural and political ideas, ricocheting against the boundaries of empire, slavery, religious dogma, and racial ideologies.

In their time, and until the twentieth century, ideas imported from abroad and transplanted to African soil faced scrutiny, and were rarely accepted at face value. This was an engaged culture, where indigenes used their home-grown ideas and practices to measure and assess new items, crops, speech patterns, and ideologies. All strangers to the Mina (Gold) Coast shared an obsession with the rightness of their theologies—dogmas inextricably filled with political, military, and commercial overtones. This assortment mirrored trade goods, where less desirable and worthless items were packaged with more desirable commodities. Of course, the three women and their people were free to choose, but the choices were not made in freedom. Choice and desire were framed by the packaging, the constraints of competition and multiple European competitors, and the overlay of acquiescence in one sort of Christian ideology or the other. What is both remarkable and ironic, then, is that what Graça, Mónica, and Adwoa refused to accept from the foreigners is now irrefutable in the present among their heirs. Revolutionaries in the ordinary, tactful, and resolute, they were committed to the power of ideas anchored in culture, in land, and in peoples unconquered. These are the ways I have come to know them and their world, and they may tell us much that we have forgotten about the shape of our own times.

Before the late nineteenth century, strangers in the role of captains, merchants, clerics, and residents could only wish for "the conversion of the [African], with zealous prayer and translation of the Bible, especially the New Testament, into the [Akan/Twi] language. Thus several hundred Moors might be converted to Christianity and in turn be confirmed as preachers among their people."[1] These words were penned by a German-speaking Lutheran pastor about the women's homeland decades after Adwoa's probable death. What has survived from this pastor is an exchange between him and unnamed indigenes, from villages where our three women lived or spent time. For all we know, they might have been kinfolk.

The pastor wrote: "If one tells them of the wonders which God performed long ago in the Old Testament, they immediately ask how many years ago it was that such wonders occurred—as if to say, 'if such long time has passed, how can one actually know such things?"

"Others can tell of wonders which ... their supposed *obossum* [*ɔbosom*] and patron saint has performed, since they have not only heard such wonders narrated by their fathers, but have in part (so they claim) witnessed them."

"If one speaks to them of God, of the Godhead, in particular of Christ, ... then one hears the blind people say all kinds of insulting and mocking things."

Somewhat undeterred, the pastor pressed on: "Concerning the conception and birth of Our Savior, Jesus Christ ... they consider it impossible that a woman can become pregnant without the action of man and give birth without losing her virginity."

"Of all the articles of belief which we Christians acknowledge with heart and mouth, the article of Christ's resurrection seems to these blind people particularly absurd and ridiculous."

"If one talks to them of Christ's resurrection, namely that on the third day he rose again from the dead, some of them consider it an impossibility and laugh at it. Others say it is nothing new, as there have been plenty of examples among them, the heathen, of people who had been killed and had come back alive again from the dead."

Doctrinally frustrated and intellectually defeated, the pastor surmised all this was "foolish talk." But he was dealing with uncolonized, sovereign, and not yet seduced peoples. This evocative exchange took place between Christian Europe and an Africa filled with its own spiritual succor, agile and able to land its own knockout punch. We might call this spiritual culture "black women power" or its equivalent during the sixteenth-century world of Graça, Mónica, and Adwoa. In either case, seduction would set in; the stranger's dogma would gain traction among enough "confirmed as preachers," operating like viruses in search of hosts, turning the immune system—that spiritual culture—against itself. The cancer was always there, on the coast, near the trading posts erected by Portuguese, Dutch, English, French, German (Brandenburg), Danish, and Swedish intruders. Within each seduced indigene, a host cell emerged, infecting others. The conquest which Adwoa and her people had rebuffed took hold along patches of her coast in the late nineteenth century. Then, the cancer began to spread.[2]

The dispersal of the strangers' ideologies was allied to the cancerous growth of maize, involving the advent of foreign starches and the loss of a balanced, pescatarian diet. Portugal fed its empire a diet of Mina gold and offered maize and further starches at the start of the sixteenth century. Neither Graça, Mónica, nor Adwoa could have imagined that the maize adapted to their climate and diet would become the most produced grain in the world. Maize fed and continues to feed humans, animals, automobiles, and a starch-based transnational diet responsible for nutritional diseases in westernizing and urbanizing regions of Africa and its diasporas.

The cast of diseases is familiar: hypertension, diabetes, obesity, cardiovascular disease, renal failure, and coronary heart disease. Poverty, marginalization, racial stratification and violence, and socio-political inequities advance them, further aided by diets of animal fats, starches, refined and processed foods, and low intake of fiber, fruits, and vegetables. Western Africa suffers from undernutrition and nutritional deficiencies, African diasporas in the Caribbean and Latin America from undernutrition and obesity, and diasporic Africans in the United States and western Europe from caloric excess, diets high in fats and processed foods, and the predominance of cheap and unwholesome food-like substances. The pace and pervasiveness of obesity, diabetes, hypertension, coronary heart disease, and certain cancers follow a transatlantic gradient from western Africa to the Americas and to Europe, in which the rate and health consequences of those diseases increase as one moves along this transatlantic route.[3]

As Graça's, Mónica's, and Adwoa's balanced diet showed, approaches to food production, combination, and preparation lie at the heart of our world's nutritional and disease profile. The road ahead, begun by their challenge to empire, suggests contesting foods of dubious nutritional value and the corporate empires that have patented the genetic make-up of crops and monopolized the arable lands on which they grow. To this we can add monocropping of hybrid maize for national and international markets; and the great emphasis on homogeneous maize-based diets, which are replacing diverse forms of food supply and nutrition with increased monotony in food production and consumption. We know reduced food diversity and increased mono-cropping weaken the resilience of our food supply and our bodies. Crops, lands, and humans become vulnerable to plant and human disease outbreaks, drought, climate change, and unprecedented human mobility. We have migrated far from these African women's dietary world, and our prevailing modes of food production flow out of factories rather than farms, where food-like edibles trump "real" food, and biodiversity, if not human diversity in form and idea, faces elimination.[4]

Graça, Mónica, and Adwoa were three magical winds that blew through the world of slaving, religious, and racial empires. Empires are allergic to endurance. Their capitalism clothed as trade created the captive, then the worker of our time. Race organized captives-turned-workers through ideologies, or plain dogmas, into hierarchies. Slavery was necessary but insufficient for racial and theological capitalism to persist, and so it morphed onward. Capitalist economies and racial ideologies are belief systems; without believers, they collapse. It was these subtle yet powerful understandings that our three women reached out to and touched. Counterintuitively, they would not have viewed Portugal's current poverty, stark income in equality, and indebtedness in Europe with any irony; its nationals came to their homeland precisely because of impoverishment in the late fifteenth century. Neither might they have found it ironic that while their sixteenth-century Africa had two polities whose rulers claimed the stranger's theology—Aksum/Ethiopia and the Kingdom of Kôngo—now the continent rivals or surpasses the number of believers in Europe.

For much of Africa, rapid growth in believers got under way in the late nineteenth century; the accelerant was colonial rule in all its inquisitional terror. Proselytizing on the Mina (Gold) Coast remained futile for four centuries, bearing fruit in the widest sense only under British colonial rule, in two generations. What was the difference? The answer is sufficient converts seduced by the taste of European goods, ideologies of civilization and modernity, and a militarized prowess propping up assertions that Europeans/whites possessed the "true" and only idea of god.

The strangers' theology rarely visited alone; it was always packaged in schooling, literacy, medical care, and morals, then distributed to potential converts who were promised a subservient place in the service of a Christian empire. To be sure, critical masses had to accept two mutually reinforcing arguments: first, they were required to opt out of their mind and humanity, believing they had wrong beliefs and were inhuman as a result; second, they were expected to believe that they could only be human, civilized, and modern under the *only* god and *his* empire.

Critical food challenges and overdoses of foreign debt and foreign faiths now pound the motherland. One feels unsurprised that nineteen of the twenty lowest-ranking countries on the human development index or most of the world's countries with the lowest life expectancies and highest death rates are African nations with significant Christian claimants. One direct implication for writers and those who take an interest in Africa is the question of whose layer of the story should reach print and be celebrated at the expense of *complete* stories. There is a telling storyline that jumps at us from the Kingdom of Kôngo, in west-central Africa. Scholars and museum curators know in grisly detail of a region ravaged by the most predacious slaving, wars, droughts, and sustained imperialism from Europe, yet the celebration of this kingdom as a Christian one belies the carnage. Even if more than royal or leading families became Christians, it is difficult to come to terms with a Christian kingdom cannibalized by ruling factions and by Catholic merchants and clerics at the cost of millions of people lost without mourning. For, as in other patches of the continent, the stranger's theology that landed in the Kôngo tied itself intimately to political and military imperatives but became the country's undoing. Theirs is a region whose current ravages of civil war, Christian profession, and food and human insecurity can be traced to the sixteenth century, when, in Chinua Achebe's celebrated idiom, things began to fall apart. What should not be lost is that this century also belonged to Graça, Mónica, and Adwoa, and theirs is a wide-angled story to be counted among, if not to counter, the rest.

NOTES

INTRODUCTION

1. I use the lower-case "god" to emphasize varying ideas and the diverse peoples who ascribed meaning to what is essentially a common noun. This approach works to destabilize a specific ownership of this common noun. Hence, it remains uncapitalized throughout the book, except in direct quotations or in sources which used the capitalized version. For the quoted statements, see Agostinho da Conceição, *Sermam do glorioso lusitano S. Antonio, prégado no seu mesmo dia, & Convento em a cidade do Rio de Janeiro, a 13. de Junho de 1674* (Lisbon: Na Officina de Antonio Rodriguez d'Abreu, 1675), 18. The Portuguese empire is similar to the British empire of the nineteenth century in the way Christian ideology was a central part of imperial identity. For the British empire, see Hilary M. Carey, *God's Empire: Religion and Colonialism in the British World, c.1801–1908* (New York: Cambridge University Press, 2011).
2. A. C. de C. M. Saunders, *A Social History of Black Slaves and Freedmen in Portugal, 1441–1555* (New York: Cambridge University Press, 1982), 145; Accounts of João do Porto, 27 February 1500, in Anselmo Braamcamp Freire, "Cartas de quitação," *Arquivo Histórico Português* 3, no. 404 (1905): 477;

António Brásio, ed., *Monumenta Missionaria Africana: Africa Occidental* (Lisbon: Agência Geral do Ultramar, Divisão de Publicações e Biblioteca, 1952–88), 1: 210–14 (henceforth, *MMA*). In the past four decades, the study of global and slaving empires has been shaped by ideological confusion, abstract "big data" coveted by economists, equally abstract linguistic conceptualizations, and the search for sources seasoned with African voices. Though ideology drove and still drives scholarly output, ideology alone has hardly advanced our understanding of the topic. Economic studies of slaveries have done more to quantify the "nefarious trade" into usable data sets, enriching while also limiting recent scholarship. Data sets say very little about the lived experiences behind their numbers. According to the premier database for transatlantic slaving, the Trans-Atlantic Slave Trade Database (TSTD), there are no numbers for the mid-to-late-fifteenth-century slaving between Iberia and Atlantic Africa at a time when Iberia claimed a monopoly. According to the TSTD, there are only fourteen recorded voyages for the period 1500–1540. All were conducted by Portuguese slavers and vessels but most disembarked at major ports in Spanish America. Only two of the fourteen voyages disembarked in Europe—one in Portugal and the other in Spain. In all forty-nine recorded voyages to Europe from Africa between 1500 and 1750, the vast majority went to Portugal and then Spain, with only three to France. We know next to nothing about African lives on African as well as European soil for either the fourteen voyages between the first four decades of the sixteenth century or the forty-nine voyages for the first two and a half centuries of Atlantic slaving to Europe—more precisely, Iberia. The stories of Graça, Mónica, and Adwoa place faces on those isolated and abstract numbers, and signify how globalizing their societies were in formative eras of an interconnected world. On these issues, see Joseph E. Inikori, "Ideology versus the Tyranny of Paradigm:

Historians and the Impact of the Atlantic Slave Trade on African Societies," *African Economic History* 22 (1994): 37–58; David Eltis and David Richardson, *Atlas of the Transatlantic Slave Trade* (New Haven, CT: Yale University Press, 2010); David Eltis and David Richardson, eds., *Extending the Frontiers: Essays on the New Transatlantic Slave Trade Database* (New Haven, CT: Yale University Press, 2008); James A. Rawley and Stephen D. Behrendt, *The Transatlantic Slave Trade: A History* (Lincoln: University of Nebraska Press, 2005); David Eltis, Stephen D. Behrendt, David Richardson, and Herbert S. Klein, *The Trans-Atlantic Slave Trade: A Database on CD-ROM* (New York: Cambridge University Press, 1999); Patrick Manning, *Slavery and African Life: Occidental, Oriental, and African Slave Trades* (New York: Cambridge University Press, 1990); David Henige, "Measuring the Immeasurable: The Atlantic Slave Trade, West African Population and the Pyrrhonian Critic," *Journal of African History* 27, no. 2 (1986): 295–313; Paul E. Lovejoy, "The Volume of the Atlantic Slave Trade: A Synthesis," *Journal of African History* 23, no. 4 (1982): 473–501; Gwendolyn Midlo Hall, "Africa and Africans in the African Diaspora: The Uses of Relational Databases," *American Historical Review* 115, no. 1 (2010): 136–50.

3. See Mariana P. Candido and Adam Jones, eds., *African Women in the Atlantic World: Property, Vulnerability and Mobility, 1660–1880* (Woodbridge, UK: Boydell and Brewer, 2019).

4. On miscegenation, see Isabel C. Henriques, "Ser escravos em S. Tomé no séculos XVI: Uma outra leitura de um mesmo quotidiano," *Revista Internacional de Estudos Africanos* 6–7 (1987): 182.

5. Nwando Achebe's "female power" is useful here to emphasize how African women exercised power separate from European or African men and in a variety of ways. See Nwando Achebe, *Female Monarchs and Merchant Queens in Africa* (Athens: Ohio University Press, 2020).

6. The principal sources for the life stories of Graça, Mónica, and Adwoa are these: Arquivo Nacional da Torre do Tombo (ANTT), Tribunal do Santo Ofício (TSO), Inquisição de Lisboa (IL), processo (proc.) 11041; ANTT, TSO, IL, proc. 12431; Biblioteca Nacional de Portugal, Fundo Geral, Mss. 8457; see also Brásio, *MMA*, 3: 89–113. The histories of these women sit within a wider literature on women and gender in African and world history. See, for instance, Kathleen Sheldon, *African Women: Early History to the 21st Century* (Bloomington: Indiana University Press, 2017); Paul Tiyambe Zeleza, "Gender Biases in African Historiography," in *African Gender Studies: A Reader*, ed. Oyèrónké Oyèwùmí (New York: Palgrave Macmillan, 2005); Bonnie G. Smith, ed., *Women's History in Global Perspective*, 3 vols. (Urbana: University of Illinois Press, 2004), specifically Cheryl Johnson-Odim's essay, "Women and Gender in the History of Sub-Saharan Africa," in *Women's History in Global Perspective*, ed. Bonnie G. Smith (Urbana: University of Illinois Press, 2004), 3: 9–67; Iris Berger and E. Frances White, *Women in Sub-Saharan Africa: Restoring Women to History* (Bloomington: Indiana University Press, 1999); Catherine Coquery-Vidrovitch, *African Women: A Modern History*, trans. Beth Gillian Raps (Boulder, CO: Westview, 1997), originally published as *Les Africaines: Histoire des femmes d'Afrique noire du XIX au XX siècle* (Paris: Éditions Desjonquères, 1994); Ayesha M. Imam, Amina Mama, and Fatou Sow, eds., *Engendering African Social Sciences* (Dakar, Senegal: CODESRIA, 1997); Oyèrónké Oyèwùmí, *The Invention of Women: Making an African Sense of Western Gender Discourses* (Minneapolis: University of Minnesota Press, 1997); Claire C. Robertson, "Never Underestimate the Power of Women: The Transforming Vision of African Women's History," *Women's Studies International Forum* 11, no. 5 (1988): 439–53; Claire C. Robertson and Martin A. Klein, eds., *Women and Slavery in Africa* (Madison: University of

Wisconsin Press, 1983); Nancy J. Hafkin and Edna G. Bay, eds., *Women in Africa: Studies in Social and Economic Change* (Stanford, CA: Stanford University Press, 1976).

7. On the concept of "racial capitalism," credited to Cedric Robinson, see Cedric J. Robinson, *On Racial Capitalism, Black Internationalism, and Cultures of Resistance*, ed. H. L. T. Quan (London: Pluto Press, 2019); Jodi Melamed, "Racial Capitalism," *Critical Ethnic Studies* 1, no. 1 (2015): 76–85; Cedric J. Robinson, *Black Marxism: The Making of the Black Radical Tradition* (Chapel Hill: University of North Carolina Press, 2000).

8. Initially called the Roman fathers, the Jesuits were a globally focused organization based in Italy though dominated by Spaniards. See Dauril Alden, *The Making of an Enterprise: The Society of Jesus in Portugal, Its Empire, and Beyond, 1540–1750* (Stanford, CA: Stanford University Press, 1996), 25. The Jesuits' increasing power, including cultural influence emanating from their missionary work overseas, brought them into conflict with European monarchs and the pope, who, in unison, suppressed or expelled the Jesuits from their domains in the eighteenth century. On the history of the Jesuits, see Thomas Worcester, ed., *The Cambridge Companion to the Jesuits* (New York: Cambridge University Press, 2008); Joseph A. Gagliano and Charles E. Ronan, eds., *Jesuit Encounters in the New World: Jesuit Chroniclers, Geographers, Educators and Missionaries in the Americas, 1549–1767* (Rome: Institutum Historicum Societatis Iesu, 1997); William V. Bangert, *A History of the Society of Jesus* (St. Louis: Institute of Jesuit Sources, 1986). On the Portuguese Asian trade, see James C. Boyajian, *Portuguese Trade in Asia under the Habsburgs, 1580–1640* (Baltimore: Johns Hopkins University Press, 2007).

9. Toby Green, *Inquisition: The Reign of Fear* (New York: Thomas Dunne Books and St. Martin's Press, 2007), 7. For all its admirable qualities, Green's book, like Stuart B. Schwartz's *All Can*

Be Saved, represents an unfortunate trend in so-called Atlantic history: there is comparatively little to no coverage of Africa (except Cape Verde) and Africans in their accounts, which focus principally on inquisitional activities in Iberia and "Latin America" with minor attention to Goa, India.

10. Alden, *Making of an Enterprise*, 670–71; Francisco Bethencourt, *The Inquisition: A Global History 1478–1834*, trans. Jean Birrell (New York: Cambridge University Press, 2009), 63; António José Saraiva, *The Marrano Factory: The Portuguese Inquisition and Its New Christians 1536–1765*, trans. and ed. Herman Prins Salomon and Isaac S. D. Sassoon (Leiden: Brill, 2001), 45, 50, 57–60; Saunders, *A Social History of Black Slaves and Freedmen in Portugal*, 159; José Lourenço D. de Mendoça and António Joaquim Moreira, *História dos principais actos e procedimentos da Inquisição em Portugal* (Lisbon: Casa da Moeda, 1980); I. S. Revah, "L'installation de l'Inquisition à Coimbra en 1541 et le premier règlement du Saint-Office portugais," *Bulletin des Études Portugaises* 27 (1966): 47–88. For recent trends in the study of the Portuguese Inquisition, see Giuseppe Marcocci, "Toward a History of the Portuguese Inquisition: Trends in Modern Historiography," *Revue de l'Histoire des Religions* 227 (2010): 355–93. More generally, see Giuseppe Marcocci and José Pedro Paiva, *História da Inquisição Portuguesa, 1536–1821* (Lisbon: A Esfera dos Livros, 2013); Francisco Bethencourt, *História das Inquisições: Portugal, Espanha, Itália* (Lisbon: Círculo de Leitores, 1994). More generally, see Green, *Inquisition*.

11. For a useful discussion of issues related to women and the archives of Christian institutions, see the introduction to Sandra Lauderdale Graham's *Caetana Says No: Women's Stories from a Brazilian Slave Society* (New York: Cambridge University Press, 2002). See also Philippe Buc's excellent account of Christian theology and violence in *Holy War, Martyrdom, and Terror: Christianity, Violence, and the West* (Philadelphia:

University of Pennsylvania Press, 2015). My approach to the Portuguese empire differs significantly from the standard "seaborne empire" accounts. See, for instance, A. R. Disney, *A History of Portugal and the Portuguese Empire*, vol. 1: *From Beginnings to 1807* (New York: Cambridge University Press, 2009); A. J. R. Russell-Wood, *The Portuguese Empire, 1415–1808: A World on the Move* (Baltimore: Johns Hopkins University Press, 1998); Bailey W. Diffie and George D. Winius, *Foundations of the Portuguese Empire, 1415–1580* (Minneapolis: University of Minnesota Press, 1977); Charles R. Boxer, *The Portuguese Seaborne Empire, 1415–1825* (New York: A. A. Knopf, 1969); Charles R. Boxer, *Four Centuries of Portuguese Expansion, 1415–1825: A Succinct Survey* (Berkeley: University of California Press, 1961).

12. While an individual's experience is private—removed from inspection—it is also not and cannot be fully representative, for lived experience and personal history are particular, providing no unique source of revelation. However, having the three women's lives both standing alone and considered together with their times, ricocheting against each other and various other people, does give us some sense of broader patterns of ideas and behaviors. These broader patterns and behaviors are the bricks and mortar of human history, and they do not require a particular, subjective position as a "black woman" or a woman's way of knowing, which is to say (falsely) that only such women can understand the category of women to which they belong. This position, a core tenet of intersectionality, is not an argument about women's experiences or histories but rather an ideological position in search of theoretical justification. Instead of fulfilling the promise of redressing the limits of "race" and "gender," the vogue academic product called intersectionality fractures race and gender identities, creating yet another category that explains extraordinarily little in real, practical ways. Graça, Mónica,

and Adwoa lived in a time when these trends did not exist, and so it would be an unproductive imposition to use any of them to interpret their lives.

13. Kiera Lindsey, "'Deliberate Freedom': Using Speculation and Imagination in Historical Biography," *TEXT: Journal of Writing and Writing Programs* 50 (2018): 1–16. For women in Europe, however, much more has been done with scant and fuller records for the fourteenth to the eighteenth centuries. See, for instance, Maria Agren, ed., *Making a Living, Making a Difference: Women and Work in Early Modern European Society* (New York: Oxford University Press, 2017); Olwen Hufton, *The Prospect Before Her: A History of Women in Western Europe, 1500–1800* (London: HarperCollins, 1995). For supposed issues of "the archive" and fictionalizing to "recover" enslaved African women's lives, see Marisa Fuentes, *Dispossessed Lives: Enslaved Women, Violence, and the Archive* (Philadelphia: University of Pennsylvania Press, 2016). A fuller discussion of the problems which this work and others like it present—stated in the text and in the endnotes—is found in chapter 3, on Adwoa's story.

14. On the male production of history, see, for instance, Monica Hesse, "Centuries of male-dominated history brought us here. How do we get everyone to accept that?," *Washington Post*, August 9, 2018; Andrew Kahn and Rebecca Onion, "Is History Written about Men, by Men?," *Slate*, January 6, 2016; Katherine Mangan, "In the Humanities, Men Dominate the Fields of Philosophy and History," *Chronicle of Higher Education*, October 29, 2012.

15. ANTT, TSO, IL, proc. 11041, f. 19r; John Vogt, *Portuguese Rule on the Gold Coast* (Athens: University of Georgia Press, 1979), 91–92. See also Natalie Zemon Davis, *Women on the Margins: Three Seventeenth-Century Lives* (Cambridge: Harvard University Press, 1995). Davis's three women, unlike Graça, Mónica, and Adwoa, lived supposedly on the margins

in seventeenth-century Europe, and in North and South America, where two of them traveled and lived. They, unlike the three women featured in this book, left behind memoirs and writings; their stories focus on childrearing, religion, literature, and relations to men. Davis's three subjects, however, took part in and reaped benefits from European colonization of the Americas, placing them far from the margins. The two in the Americas, Marie and Maria, had access to money and other resources, and assumed colonial power in relation to indigenes, who occupied subjugated roles as laborers, servants, and converts. Marie and Maria's treks across the Atlantic, unlike the journeys of Graça and Mónica, who traveled the Atlantic as prisoners, followed the path of powerful European men who engaged in colonization, and their ambitions and social positions matched those of their male counterparts. Thus, though non-elite in Europe, they were elite in the Americas, as well as literate and well-read women. Traveling the Atlantic as a prisoner in the forging of the "modern world" represented—for Graça, Mónica, and millions to follow—a severance rather than the ubiquitous connections stressed in Atlantic world scholarship. For Graça, Mónica, and Adwoa, the "Atlantic world" was peripheral to their lives.

16. For a recent book that takes up the farcical story of freedom among African women and women of African ancestry in the so-called Atlantic world, see Jessica Marie Johnson, *Wicked Flesh: Black Women, Intimacy, and Freedom in the Atlantic World* (Philadelphia: University of Pennsylvania Press, 2020).

1. "A RENEGADE FROM THE CATHOLIC FAITH"

1. For Graça's case file, see Arquivo Nacional da Torre do Tombo (ANTT), Tribunal do Santo Ofício (TSO), Inquisição de Lisboa (IL), processo (proc.) 11041. The quotation is from

folio (f.) 26v. Graça's case started out within the framework of the bishop's court (*Ordinário*), and at a later stage representatives of the Inquisition were called in as the accusation touched on issues of faith, that is, heresy; the final sentence was handed down by representatives from both the Inquisition and the bishop's court. This very early case came before the Inquisition had worked out what was to become its usual procedure in so-called witchcraft cases. Unlike the Spanish Inquisition, the Portuguese one worked out an informal division of labor with the ordinary church justice system (bishop's courts, as opposed to inquisitional ones, which were under the dual jurisdiction of the Church and the Crown), whereby the Inquisition dealt with cases where formal heresy was involved (e.g. Judaism, Lutheranism, Islam), leaving so-called minor offenses (blasphemy, superstition, etc.) to bishop's courts. Witchcraft was a borderline case: if it involved an explicit or implicit pact with the Devil, it was for the Inquisition; if not, it stayed in the church courts. In sixteenth-century cases there are a few references to Africa, mostly in early trials for Islam or smuggling. The latter cases are curious: since, for instance, selling horses or cloth to North Africa was equivalent to selling strategic weapons to the (religious) enemy, the king of Portugal determined that smugglers to North Africa be tried by the Inquisition. Since enslaved Africans charged with witchcraft were unlikely to have been involved in worship of the Christian Devil, their cases were usually tried by the bishop's courts.

2. Dauril Alden, *The Making of an Enterprise: The Society of Jesus in Portugal, Its Empire, and Beyond, 1540–1750* (Stanford, CA: Stanford University Press, 1996), 26–27 (quotation), 37, 673; Giuseppe Marcocci, "Toward a History of the Portuguese Inquisition: Trends in Modern Historiography (1974–2009)," *Revue de l'Histoire des Religions* 3 (2010): 355–93; Giuseppe Marcocci, "A fundação da Inquisição em Portugal: Um novo olhar," *Lusitania Sacra* 23 (2011): 17–40. According to

Marcocci, leading officials of the Spanish Inquisition applied pressure on the Portuguese Crown so that the latter would prosecute "New Christians," or converted Jews and Muslims. Added to this mix was a new group of theological councilors joining João III's court in the late 1520s and the start of the 1530s, staging a fight between João III, the corrupt world of the administrative unit that aided the pope in governing the Catholic world, and diplomatic efforts of New Christian agents in Rome. Manuel's claims to newly "discovered" lands were confirmed by the papacy and recognized by the Spanish, and so Manuel maintained close relations. Manuel first married Isabella, eldest daughter of co-sovereigns Ferdinand and Isabella and widow of João II's heir. As a condition of the marriage, Manuel was to expel the Jews, many thousands of whom had been admitted by João II after their expulsion from Spain in 1492. In December 1496 Manuel ordered Jews and free Muslims to leave Portugal within ten months. On their assembly in Lisbon, attempts were made to force their conversion. Some were allowed to leave, but the rest were "converted" under the promise that no inquiry should be made into their beliefs for thirty years. Manuel also exempted the Church and the military orders of knighthood from certain obligations. He severely punished those responsible for the massacre of Jews in 1506. In the previous year he had decreed that Castilians who were not condemned by Castile's Inquisition and wished to live in Portugal had to present themselves in the first forty days to the factor of the Casa da Mina, to be registered and to buy there a thousand gold *cruzados* of spices and acquire cattle. Castilians already resident in Portugal illegally would be pardoned once they fulfilled the same conditions. Nonetheless, Manuel's hope for a male child to rule Portugal and Spain was dashed when he married Eleanor of Austria, sister of the emperor Charles V, in 1518. Only one daughter came out of this marriage, then Manuel died in December 1521. On

Manuel's 1505 royal decree, see Maria Luisa Oliveira Esteves, ed., *Portugaliae Monumenta Africana* (Lisbon: Comissão Nacional das Comemorações dos Descobrimentos Portugueses; Imprensa Nacional—Casa da Moeda, 1993), 5: 92–93. As for the Jesuits, the first ones in Portugal were Francis Xavier and Simão Rodrigues, who were companions of St. Ignatius of Loyola. Ignatius and Xavier were students in Paris, then ordained as priests in Venice in 1537. In September 1539, Pope Paul III verbally approved the establishment of the Society of Jesus as a religious order. The next year, after Xavier had arrived in Lisbon en route to India, the pope signed a papal bull officially creating the Society and assigned to it a small church in the heart of Rome. Xavier left after one year for India, and Rodrigues became the founder of the Jesuit Order under João III. In the papal bull establishing the Portuguese Inquisition, the pope appointed three bishops and a General or Grand Inquisitor, but only Diogo da Silva accepted the appointment. The pope allowed the Portuguese monarch to appoint a fourth General Inquisitor. In 1539, João III forced the bishop of Ceuta and royal confessor, Diogo da Silva, to renounce his position as General Inquisitor of the Lisbon tribunal. Cardinal and brother of João III, Dom Henrique became the new General Inquisitor. From 1539 onward the king named the new General Inquisitor, the one the pope allowed him to choose. And it remained this way. With the heads of the Inquisition and the monarchy aligned, João III was anxious to recruit the Jesuits before papal approval. When the opportunity presented itself, he directed his ambassador, Pedro Mascarenhas, to urge the pope to approve the establishment of the Society of Jesus. In 1546, the province of Portugal was established as the first in the Society with Rodrigues as its first head. Two years later, the first Jesuits went to the kingdom of Kôngo. Before long, Portugal became the Jesuit nursery, producing and dispatching hundreds of priests to the far reaches of the empire. A

1561–62 survey among recruits, however, showed that more than half were more concerned with their own souls than the welfare of others, and that few desired to be "soul curers" in the colonial outposts of the empire; despite some feuding, the Jesuits aided and abetted the Inquisition.

3. Bryan Givens, *Judging Maria de Macedo: A Female Visionary and the Inquisition in Early Modern Portugal* (Baton Rouge: Louisiana State University Press, 2011), 16–17.

4. Giuseppe Marcocci, "Blackness and Heathenism: Color, Theology, and Race in the Portuguese World, c.1450–1600," *Anuario Colombiano de Historia Social y de la Cultura* 43, no. 2 (2016): 33–57; Giuseppe Marcocci, "Saltwater Conversion: Trans-Oceanic Sailing and Religious Transformation in the Iberian World," in *Space and Conversion in Global Perspective*, eds. Giuseppe Marcocci, Aliocha Maldavsky, Wietse de Boer, and Ilaria Pavan (Leiden: Brill, 2014), 251–52; A. C. De C. M. Saunders, *A Social History of Black Slaves and Freedmen in Portugal, 1441–1555* (New York: Cambridge University Press, 1982), 161; David Birmingham, "The Regimento da Mina," *Transactions of the Historical Society of Ghana* 11 (1970): 2–3; Archivo General de Indias, Sevilla, Audiencia de Mexico, legajo 3177, exp. 4, capitulos de una carta del Virrey sobre diezmos y edificacion de yglesias, 6 March 1534, f. 2v. The original and partial English translation can be found in University of New Mexico, Center for Southwest Research, Mss. 769, box 5, folder 28.

5. ANTT, TSO, IL, proc. 11041, ff. 2–3r; Esteves, *Portugaliae Monumenta Africana*, 2: 438–72; J. Bato'ora Ballong-Wen-Mewuda, *São Jorge da Mina, 1482–1637: La vie d'un comptoir portugais en Afrique occidentale* (Lisbon: Fondation Calouste Gulbenkian, 1993), 2: 507.

6. On literacy rates in Europe, see E. Buringh and J. L. van Zanden, "Charting the 'Rise of the West': Manuscripts and Printed Books in Europe, a Long-Term Perspective from the

Sixth through Eighteenth Centuries," *Journal of Economic History* 69, no. 2 (2009): 409–45. Mid-sixteenth-century France led the way with an eighteen or nineteen per cent literacy rate; no or insufficient data exist for Portugal, but it is probably higher than Sweden's one per cent but lower than half of France's rate.

7. John Vogt, "Private Trade and Slave Sales at São Jorge da Mina: A Fifteenth-Century Document," *Transactions of the Historical Society of Ghana* 15, no. 1 (1974): 110 (unlabeled table).

8. J. D. M. Ford, ed., *Letters of John III, King of Portugal, 1521–1557* (Cambridge, MA: Harvard University Press, 1931), 3.

9. See Marcocci, "Blackness and Heathenism." Marcocci argues convincingly for the unsettled nature of early Portuguese input in shaping modern racist thought, while avoiding a teleological approach to the topic. Though he is guilty of using such an approach, see the useful discussion in James H. Sweet, "The Iberian Roots of American Racist Thought," *William and Mary Quarterly* 54 (1997): 143–66.

10. António Brásio, ed., *Monumenta Missionaria Africana* (Lisbon: Agência Geral do Ultramar, 1952–1988), 3: 90–91 (henceforth, *MMA*).

11. A. Teixeira da Mota and P. E. H. Hair, *East of Mina: Afro-European Relations on the Gold Coast in the 1550s and 1560s* (Madison: University of Wisconsin, African Studies Program, 1988), 86.

12. John Vogt, *Portuguese Rule on the Gold Coast* (Athens: University of Georgia Press, 1979), 46; John Vogt, "The Early São Tomé–Principe Slave Trade with Mina, 1500–1540," *International Journal of African Historical Studies* 11, no. 3 (1973): 454; Vogt, "Private Trade," 104–6; John Vogt, "Portuguese Gold Trade: An Account Ledger from Elmina, 1529–1531," *Transactions of the Historical Society of Ghana* 14, no. 1 (1973): 96; A. Teixeira da Mota, *Some Aspects of*

Portuguese Colonisation and Sea Trade in West Africa in the 15th and 16th Centuries (Bloomington: African Studies Program, Indiana University, 1978), 10; Birmingham, "The Regimento da Mina," 2.

13. ANTT, Corpo Cronológico (CC), parte 2, mç. 85, no. 75.

14. Ruth Lawlor has argued, "The raped woman is *always* a victim in such archives" (emphasis added). I am not convinced Graça or any of the women in this book would agree with that claim. See Ruth Lawlor, "Working with Death: The Experience of Feeling in the Archive," *Perspectives on History* 59 (2021): 17.

15. Pieter de Marees, *Description and Historical Account of the Gold Kingdom of Guinea (1602)*, ed. and trans. Albert van Dantzig and Adam Jones (London: British Academy, 1987), 40.

16. De Marees, *Description*, 41. The Vale do Zebro (Barreiro), south of Lisbon, was the place since the fifteenth century where the king's biscuit ovens were located. See *MMA*, 15: 8.

17. ANTT, CC, parte 1, mç. 9, no. 61 (2 September 1510); Giovanni Ramusio, *Delle navigationi et viaggi nel qual si contiene la descrittione dell'Africa* (Venice: Lucantonio Giunti, 1550), 1: 126–28. See also John W. Blake, *Europeans in West Africa, 1450–1560* (London: The Hakluyt Society, 1941–42), 1: 149; Kwasi Konadu, *The Akan Diaspora in the Americas* (New York: Oxford University Press, 2010), 31–32. For a discussion of these innovations, see James D. La Fleur, *Fusion Foodways of Africa's Gold Coast in the Atlantic Era* (Leiden: Brill, 2012).

18. Mota and Hair, *East of Mina*. On maize in Africa and along the Mina (Gold) Coast, see James C. McCann, *Maize and Grace: A History of Africa's Encounter with a New World Crop* (Cambridge, MA: Harvard University Press, 2005); La Fleur, *Fusion Foodways of Africa's Gold Coast in the Atlantic Era*; A. Teixeira Da Mota and A. Carreira, "'Milho Zaburro' and

'Milho Maçaroca' in Guinea and in the Islands of Cabo Verde," *Africa* 36, no. 1 (1966): 73–77; Stanley B. Alpern, "The European Introduction of Crops into West Africa in Precolonial Times," *History in Africa* 19 (1992): 24–25; Eustache Delafosse, *Voyage a la côte occidentale d'Afrique, en Portugal et en Espagne (1479–1480)*, ed. R. Foulche-Delbosc (Paris: Alfonse Picard et Fils, 1897), 12–15; P. E. H. Hair, "A Note on De La Fosse's 'Mina' Vocabulary of 1479–80," *Journal of West African Languages* 3 (1966): 55–57; David Dalby and P. E. H. Hair, "A Further Note on the Mina Vocabulary of 1479–80," *Journal of West African Languages* 5 (1968): 129. See Jean Barbot's 1680 vocabularies of four African languages (Wolof, Fula, Akan/Twi, Ewe/Fon), in P. E. H. Hair, *Barbot's West African Vocabularies of c.1680* (Liverpool: Centre of African Studies, University of Liverpool, 1992), 26; Paul Isert, *Letters on West Africa and the Slave Trade: Paul Erdmann Isert's Journey to Guinea and the Caribbean Islands in Columbia* (1788), trans. and ed. Selena A. Winsnes (New York: Oxford University Press for the British Academy, 1992), 123; Alpern, "The European Introduction of Crops into West Africa in Precolonial Times," 14–16; Sigismund Koelle, *Polyglotta Africana*, ed. P. E. H. Hair and David Dalby (Graz: Akademische Druck- und Verlagsanstalt, 1963), 109–13; Adam Jones, *German Sources for West African History, 1599–1669* (Wiesbaden: Franz Steiner Verlag, 1983), 320–22; Hans Riis, *Grammatical Outline and Vocabulary of the Oji-Language* (Basel: Bahnmaier, 1854), 139, 152, 160, 204, 247; P. E. H. Hair, "An Ethnolinguistic Inventory of the Lower Guinea Coast before 1700: Part II," *African Language Review* 8 (1968): 231, 248; J. G. Christaller, *A Dictionary of the Asante and Fante Language Called Tshi* (Basel: Evangelical Missionary Society, 1881), 17, 22, 33, 40, 54, 269, 358, 502–3, 549. See also Linda A. Newson and Susie Minchin, *From Capture to Sale: The*

Portuguese Slave Trade to Spanish South America in the Early Seventeenth Century (Leiden: Brill, 2007), 300–301; Adam Jones, ed. and trans., *West Africa in the Mid-Seventeenth Century: An Anonymous Dutch Manuscript* (Atlanta: African Studies Association Press, 1995), 220. "Jojoos" was likely a Dutch transcription of the Portuguese *feijãos* or *feijões* (beans).

19. ANTT, TSO, IL, proc. 11041, ff. 13r–19r. On Manuel de Albuquerque's family history, see Anselmo Braamcamp Freire, *Brasões da Sala de Sintra* (Coimbra: Imprensa da Universidade de Coimbra, 1927), 2: 212–13. On Captain Diogo Lopes de Sequeira, there are some discrepancies about his tenure at São Jorge da Mina. The surviving records indicate Sequeira accepted the post at the end of December 1503 and served in that capacity until 1505, but there are records of António de Miranda de Azevedo serving as captain-governor in 1504, during Sequeira's tenure. While surviving records have Azevedo there in 1504, Sequeira is captain until at least January 2, 1505, and in one source of that date D. Martinho da Silva is set to assume the captaincy after him. Finally, the italicized portions of the proceedings appear underlined in the original. Also italicized to show emphasis, though not in the original, is the phrase *And I slapped her several times to make her tell the truth.*

20. ANTT, TSO, IL, proc. 11041, ff. 19r–23r; CC, parte 2, mç. 237, no. 139; *MMA*, 15: 59, p. 139.

21. Isaías da Rosa Pereira, *Documentos para a história da Inquisição em Portugal* (Lisbon: Arquivo Histórico Dominicano Português, 1984), 79.

22. On the weather in western Europe around the mid-sixteenth century, see Thomas Short, *A General Chronological History of Air, Weather, Seasons, Meteors in Sundry Places and Different Times*, 2 vols. (London: T. Longman, 1749); Joseph Jean Nicolas Fuster, *Des changements dans le climat de la France: Histoire de ses révolutions météorologiques* (Paris: Chapelle,

1845); Franz Arago, *Sämmtliche Werke*, vol. 8 (Leipzig: Verlag von Otto Wigand, 1860); Cornelius Walford, *The Famines of the World: Past and Present* (London: Edward Stanford, 1879). The words of seventeenth-century vicar-general João Serrão were quoted in Laurinda Abreu, *The Political and Social Dynamics of Poverty, Poor Relief and Health Care in Early-Modern Portugal* (New York: Routledge, 2016), 220, but see the original in Biblioteca da Ajuda, 51-VIII-39, f. 153v.

23. The House of Catechumens was modeled after the Roman one established by St. Ignatius in 1543.

24. The Aljube was an infamous ecclesiastical prison in Lisbon until the early nineteenth century. The Aljube was also used for women accused of common crimes into the early twentieth century. See Isaías da Rosa Pereira, *Livro de receita e despesa dos presos ricos da Inquisição de Lisboa (1594–1596)* (Lisbon: Livraria Olisipo, 1994); João Brandão, *Grandeza e abastança de Lisboa em 1552*, ed. José da Felicidade Alves (Lisbon: Livros Horizonte, 1990), 160–63.

25. See Isabel dos Guimarães Sá, "Social and Religious Boundaries in Confraternities, Prisons and Hospitals in Renaissance Portugal," in *Brotherhood and Boundaries*, ed. S. Pastore, A. Prosperi, and N. Terpstra (Pisa: Edizioni della Normale, 2011), 171–89.

26. ANTT, TSO, IL, proc. 11041, ff. 20–22v. I have slightly altered the third-person speeches of each individual in Graça's trial dossier, turning them into dialogue, using the first-person voice. Thus, *she said that he* becomes *she said, "he ...."* Where underlined statements appear, and there are few, these will be emphasized as intended in the original. Finally, punctuation marks and terms indicating emotions or gestures will be made explicit in the dialogue.

27. Susana Bastos Mateus, "The Citadel of the Lost Souls: Spaces of Orthodoxy and Penance in Sixteenth-Century Lisbon," in

Space and Conversion in Global Perspective, eds. Giuseppe Marcocci, Aliocha Maldavsky, Wietse de Boer, and Ilaria Pavan (Leiden: Brill, 2014), 127–53.

28. Eduardo Freire de Oliveira, ed., *Elementos para a historia do municipio de Lisboa* (Lisbon: Tipografia Universal, 1906), 15: 386–87; *Livro do lançamento e serviço que a cidade de Lisboa fez a el Rei Nosso Senhor no ano de 1565* (Lisbon: Câmara Municipal de Lisboa, 1947), 2: 189–91. Gaspar Tibão appeared at Vilhegas's home on Saco Street, which extended over the parishes of Mártires and São Julião, now part of Serpa Pinto Street. The original Saco Street was destroyed by the great earthquake and fire of 1755. For descriptions of Saco Street (rua do Saco) in 1551–52, see Cristóvão Rodrigues de Oliveira, *Lisboa em 1551: Sumário: em que brevemente se contêm algumas coisas assim eclesiásticas como seculares que há na cidade de Lisboa* (Lisbon: Livros Horizonte, 1987), 24, 27, 76; Brandão, *Grandeza e abastança*, 168–71. For seventeenth- and eighteenth-century descriptions, see João Nunes Tinoco, *Planta da cidade de L[isbo]a em q se mostrão os muros de vermelho com todas as ruas e praças da cidade dos muros a dentro co as declarações postas em seu lugar* (Lisbon: Lithographia da Imprensa Nacional, 1853 [1650]); ANTT, Códices e documentos de proveniência desconhecida, n. 153, Livro das plantas das freguesias de Lisboa, f.43 (parish of Mártires with the rua do Saco), f. 103 (parish of Sé with the rua do Aljube). Diego Ortiz de Vilhegas was appointed bishop of São Tomé and Principe on January 31, 1533, and remained in that position until September 24, 1540, when he became the bishop of Ceuta. As bishop of São Tomé, the diocese under which Mina fell, he was succeeded by Bernardo da Cruz, who resigned on April 28, 1553. Cruz was formerly rector of the University of Coimbra and was charged by Cardinal Henrique to establish an inquisitional office in Coimbra. Vilhegas died on July 4, 1544.

29. ANTT, TSO, IL, proc. 11041, ff. 3v–5r.

30. ANTT, TSO, IL, proc. 11041, ff. 5r–7r.

31. ANTT, CC, parte 1, mç. 80, no. 74, ff. 1–2r.

32. ANTT, TSO, IL, proc. 11041, ff. 7r–9v. On bread-making, see William Rubel, *Bread: A Global History* (London: Reaktion Books, 2011).

33. ANTT, TSO, IL, proc. 11041, ff. 9v–13r.

34. ANTT, TSO, IL, proc. 11041, ff. 23r–25r.

35. ANTT, TSO, IL, proc. 11041, ff. 25r–26r. Africans were usually denounced for "sins" involving moral, sexual, or religious deviance. Though most came before the Inquisition for the last, there were other "crimes" allegedly committed by them. Before 1560, the only "black bigamists" in the records were "mulatto" or those labelled *baço* (dark) and reared in Portugal. Homosexuality was punished by time in the galleys—the Inquisition kept a special book called "Book of the Evil Sin" (*mau pecado*) listing all denounced homosexuals. See Saunders, *A Social History*, 159–60. The records for the king's attorney's response to the prosecutor are severely damaged, and the first part of it is too mangled to quote. Rather, from what I can make out, I have chosen to summarize those initial portions.

36. ANTT, TSO, IL, proc. 11041, f. 26v.

37. ANTT, TSO, IL, proc. 11041, ff. 26r–26v; Oliveira, *Lisboa em 1551*, 76. The convent is on Braun's map of Lisbon, where no. 40 (Monasterium Sanctae Clarae) is. In 1551, the convent had a hundred nuns, two chapels and a brotherhood. Though refurbished in the seventeenth century, it was completely destroyed by the 1755 fire and earthquake, and the community was then transferred to the Convento da Piedade da Esperança in Lisbon. By 1828, the convent was no longer in existence.

38. ANTT, TSO, IL, proc. 11041, f. 26r; ANTT, CC, parte 1, mç. 71, no. 37 (23 December 1541).

39. ANTT, CC, parte 2, mç. 237, no. 139; *MMA*, 15: 59, p. 139.

2. "SHE WAS MANIFESTLY DENYING THE TRUTH"

1. Arquivo Nacional da Torre do Tombo (ANTT), Tribunal do Santo Ofício (TSO), Inquisição de Lisboa (IL), processo (proc.) 12431, folios (ff.) 5r, 11r. To the best of my knowledge, the only scholarly treatment involving Mónica's case is an article by Marcus Vinicius Reis. See Marcus V. Reis, "Circulação de crenças e saberes mágico-religiosos no mundo luso-africano do século XVI: Os processos inquisitoriais de Catarina de Faria e Mônica Fernandes," *Revista Trilhas da História* 8, no. 15 (2018): 6–29.
2. ANTT, TSO, IL, proc. 12431, f. 8v. As in the case of Graça, I have slightly transformed passages where Mónica spoke into dialogue, using the first- rather than the third-person pronoun(s).
3. ANTT, TSO, IL, proc. 12431, f. 8v. Portuguese recorded the locality of present-day Axim as Axem or Achem. The Portuguese [x] has a [sh] sound, making *A-sh-em* more likely to have been Akan/Twi *Akyem*.
4. ANTT, TSO, IL, proc. 12431, f. 9r.
5. ANTT, TSO, IL, proc. 12431, f. 9v (emphasis added).
6. ANTT, TSO, IL, proc. 12431, f. 9v (emphasis added).
7. ANTT, TSO, IL, proc. 12431, f. 2r.
8. ANTT, TSO, IL, proc. 12431, f. 3r.
9. ANTT, TSO, IL, proc. 12431, ff. 3r–v, 5r.
10. ANTT, TSO, IL, proc. 12431, ff. 2r–v, 4r.
11. ANTT, TSO, IL, proc. 12431, f. 2v.
12. ANTT, TSO, IL, proc. 12431, ff. 2v–3.
13. ANTT, TSO, IL, proc. 12431, f. 3r.
14. ANTT, TSO, IL, proc. 12431, f. 3v.
15. ANTT, TSO, IL, proc. 12431, f. 3v.
16. ANTT, Corpo Cronológico (CC), parte I, maço 80, no. 74, ff. 1–2r.
17. ANTT, TSO, IL, proc. 12431, ff. 3–4, 6.

18. ANTT, TSO, IL, proc. 12431, f. 6r.
19. ANTT, TSO, IL, proc. 12431, f. 6r.
20. ANTT, TSO, IL, proc. 12431, ff. 5r–v.
21. ANTT, TSO, IL, proc. 12431, f. 6r.
22. ANTT, TSO, IL, proc. 12431, f. 6v. On Lisbon as a global city in the sixteenth century, see Annemarie Jordan-Gschwend and Kate J. P. Lowe, *The Global City: On the Streets of Renaissance Lisbon* (London: Paul Holberton Publishing, 2015).
23. ANTT, TSO, IL, proc. 12431, f. 1v. Father Master Friar Jerónimo de Azambuja, a Dominican theological scholar fluent in Greek and Hebrew but also known as a ruthless prosecutor, oversaw numerous cases while an inquisitor between 1552 and 1561. During the year of Mónica's case, he tried several. See, for instance, Cecil Roth, "The Case of Thomas Fernandes before the Lisbon Inquisition," *Miscellanies* (Jewish Historical Society of England) 2 (1935): 32–56. For a portrait of his ruthlessness and perhaps insight into his psyche, see António José Saraiva, *The Marrano Factory: The Portuguese Inquisition and Its New Christians 1536–1765*, trans. Herman Prins Salomon and Isaac S. D. Sassoon (Leiden: Brill, 2001), xiii n. 10.
24. ANTT, TSO, IL, proc. 12431, f. 10r.
25. ANTT, TSO, IL, proc. 12431, f. 10v.
26. ANTT, TSO, IL, proc. 12431, f. 10v.
27. ANTT, TSO, IL, proc. 12431, ff. 10v–11r. A notation, after Mónica was sent back to her cell, read, "And, being asked, she declared that, when she anointed herself with the said powders, she did not utter any words or perform any ceremonies" (f. 11v).
28. ANTT, TSO, IL, proc. 12431, f. 11r; ANTT, CC, parte II, maço 85, no. 75, f. 13v.
29. ANTT, TSO, IL, proc. 12431, f. 11r.
30. ANTT, TSO, IL, proc. 12431, f. 11v.

31. ANTT, TSO, IL, proc. 12431, f. 12r (emphasis added).

32. ANTT, TSO, IL, proc. 12431, ff. 12r–v.

33. ANTT, TSO, IL, proc. 12431, f. 12v.

34. ANTT, TSO, IL, proc. 12431, f. 14r.

35. ANTT, TSO, IL, proc. 12431, f. 14r.

3. "CALLED BY THEIR HEATHEN NAMES"

1. Robert S. Rattray, *Ashanti Proverbs* (Oxford: Clarendon Press, 1916), 71, 125.

2. António Brásio, ed., *Monumenta Missionaria Africana: Africa Occidental* (Lisbon: Agência Geral do Ultramar, Divisão de Publicações e Biblioteca, 1952–88), 1: 451–52. Henceforth, *MMA*.

3. Jeremiah D. M. Ford, ed., *The Letters of John III, King of Portugal, 1521–1557* (Cambridge, MA: Harvard University Press, 1931), 3–4 (emphasis added); John W. Blake, *Europeans in West Africa, 1450–1560* (London: The Hakluyt Society, 1941–2), 1: 133–35.

4. On Madu, also known as Catarina, see ANTT, TSO, IL, proc. 12431, ff. 2v–3. For a recent writer who uses fabulation and inventive tales to narrate the lives of women of African descent, see Saidiya Hartman, *Wayward Lives, Beautiful Experiments: Intimate Histories of Social Upheaval* (New York: Norton, 2019).

5. The reference to Adwoa ("Aduá") is in Biblioteca Nacional de Portugal (BNP), Fundo Geral, Mss. 8457, f. 103r. See also *MMA*, 3: 89–113. On informed speculation as a technique in historical research and writing, see J. N. P. Davies, "Informed Speculation on the Cause of Sleeping Sickness 1898–1903," *Medical History* 12, no. 2 (1968): 200–204; Natalie Zemon Davis, *The Return of Martin Guerre* (Cambridge, MA: Harvard University Press, 1983); Sudel Fuma, ed., *Mémoire orale et esclavage dans les îles du sud-ouest de l'Océan Indien: Silences, oublis, reconnaissance* (Saint Denis: CRESOI, Université de la

Réunion, 2005); Luke Pitcher, *Writing Ancient History: An Introduction to Classical Historiography* (New York: I. B. Tauris, 2009), 99; Sue Peabody, "Microhistory, Biography, Fiction: The Politics of Narrating the Lives of People under Slavery," *Transatlantica* 2 (2012), https://doi.org/10.4000/transatlantica.6184; Kiera Lindsey, "'Deliberate Freedom': Using Speculation and Imagination in Historical Biography," *TEXT: Journal of Writing and Writing Programs* 50 (2018): 1–16; Martin Duberman, *Luminous Traitor: The Just and Daring Life of Roger Casement; A Biographical Novel* (Oakland: University of California Press, 2019), 276–77.

6. Quote from Gonçalo Toscano de Almeida, Vicar of Mina, to the King, April 14, 1548, in Arquivo Nacional da Torre do Tombo (ANTT), Corpo Cronológico (CC), parte I, maço 80, no. 74, ff. 1–2r. The names were collected from the following communiques: ANTT, CC, parte 1, maço 3, no. 119; CC, parte I, maço 4, no. 32; CC, parte 2, maço 16, no. 161; CC, parte 2, maço 16, no. 30; CC, parte 1, maço 89, no. 82, CC, parte I, maço 13, no. 48; Núcleo Antigo 867, August 13, 1499; Fragmentos, Cartas para el-rei, caixa 1, maço 1, no. 9; *MMA*, 1: 130. See also Maria Emília Madeira Santos, "Rotas atlânticas: O caso da carreira de S. Tomé," in *Actas do II Colóquio Internacional de História da Madeira* (Lisbon: Instituto de Investigação Científica e Tropical, 1989), 649–55; João Martins da Silva Marques, *Descobrimentos portugueses: Documentos para a sua história* (Lisbon: Instituto para a Alta Cultura, 1971), 3: 520–41. What the Portuguese recorded as *Aheno* was the Akan leadership title *aɔhene*. For a useful discussion of *aɔhene*, see Kwasi Konadu, *Akan Pioneers: African Histories, Diasporic Experiences* (New York: Diasporic Africa Press, 2018), 43. Pieter de Marees recorded the term as *aene*, Samuel Brun as *henna*, and Wilhelm Müller as *ohinne*. See Pieter de Marees, *Description and Historical Account of the Gold Kingdom of Guinea (1602)*, ed. and trans. Albert van Dantzig and Adam Jones

(London: British Academy, 1987), 88; Adam Jones, ed., *German Sources for West African History, 1599–1669* (Wiesbaden: Steiner, 1983), 81, 298. The name Briolanja was popular in Portugal and Castile during the Middle Ages, likely on account of a character of the same name in *Amadis de Gaula*, a very popular work of literature—a chivalric romance—in sixteenth-century Iberia. The Briolanja from Adwoa's homeland was recorded at the end of the fifteenth century, before the name was in vogue. Ultimately, the name entered Spanish and Portuguese from the French *brion l'ange*; indeed, there is a village bearing the same name in France. See Marcelino Menéndez y Pelayo, *Obras completas*, vol. II: *Orígenes de la novela* (Santander: Editorial Universidad de Cantabria, 2018), 1: 224.

7. De Marees, *Description*, 23.

8. Jones, *German Sources*, 88, 109, 218.

9. Jean Barbot, "A Description of the Coasts of North and South-Guinea, 1678–88," in Awnsham Churchill, *A Collection of Voyages and Travels* ... (London: Messrs. Churchill, 1732), 244. See also P. E. H. Hair, Adam Jones, and Robin Law, eds., *Barbot on Guinea: The Writings of Jean Barbot on West Africa, 1678–1712* (London: The Hakluyt Society, 1992). Among those in Nkrān ("Accra"), Barbot observed or was told circumcision occurred "at no place on the whole coast, but only at Accra; where infants are circumcised by the priest, at the same time that they receive their names."

10. De Marees, *Description*, 23–27; Hair, Jones, and Law, *Barbot on Guinea*, 1: 130, 275; 2: 506; Jones, *German Sources*, 88. On Akan names and the calendar system that these follow, see Kwasi Konadu, *Our Own Way in This Part of the World: Biography of an African Community, Culture, and Nation* (Durham, NC: Duke University Press 2019), 63–67; Kwasi Konadu, "The Calendrical Factor in Akan History," *International Journal of African Historical Studies* 45, no. 2 (2012): 217–46.

11. Before the scheduled day of the *adintoɔ* ceremony, items such
as palm wine or an intoxicating drink (*nsa*), two cups (*nku-
ruwa*), water (*nsuo*), a mat (*kɛtɛ*), a calabash (*pakyi* or *kora*),
and a broom (*ɔprae*) would be gathered for the girl child.
Early in the morning of the scheduled day, two elders of good
character from the father's family would be sent to retrieve
Adwoa and her mother from the mother's house. One of the
elders—a woman for a girl child, and a man for a male child—
would be chosen to perform the ceremony. Adwoa's mother
would then bathe the infant and both would dress in white
cloth and stay indoors until the ceremony begun. Sacred
beads (such as *bɔdɔm*, *ahenewa*, and *abobɔe*) would be placed
on the child, and marks made with white clay (*hyire*) and specific to this ceremony would be drawn on the child and
mother. Just before daybreak, close relatives and friends of
the mother would help in the preparation, as the *adintoɔ* ceremony started with an opening libation poured by an elder
who would announce the occasion and its purpose. The family of Adwoa's mother would provide provided the drink used
for the opening libation, which would be at every doorstep
and the main entrance to the house. Adwoa would have
belonged to one of eight Akan matrilineal clans, each associated with an *akraboa* (sacred animal) and a basic character—Oyoko (falcon; patience), Asona (raven; wisdom), Asenɛɛ
(bat; diplomacy), Aduana (dog; skill), Ekoɔna (buffalo;
uprightness), Asakyiri (vulture; cleanliness), Agona (parrot;
eloquence), and Beretuo (leopard; aggressiveness). These
clans are associated with an equivalent group of stars the
Akan identify as the original ancestress (*aberewa*, "the old
woman") and her children. Nonetheless, the father's family
would provide the drink for the second libation. Afterwards,
Adwoa would be taken out of the house, stripped naked, and
then placed on a prepared area of the ground. When the
guests arrived, a female or male elder of the father would take

the child to her or his lap, and both the water and the alcoholic beverage would be poured into separate cups. The officiating elder would speak something to this effect: *Yɛbɛfrɛ wo Adwoa ne asekyerɛ din yɛ yɛwoo wo Ɛdwoada* (We will call you Adwoa and this name means your [feminine] soul decided to come to this earth on a Monday); *Ɛfiri nne rekɔ yɛbɛfrɛ wo Adwoa (agyadin)* (From today onward, we will call you Adwoa [and at least her patrilineal clan/family name—*agyadin*]). The Akan conception of a cosmic force is in step with the process of creation, and this may explain why they acknowledge first but almost never pour libations to this cosmic force. See Willem Bosman, *A New and Accurate Description of the Coast of Guinea* (London: J. Knapton, 1705), 153 (quotation). On the personal qualities of the Monday-born, among others, see Kwame Gyekye, *An Essay on African Philosophical Thought: The Akan Conceptual Scheme* (Philadelphia: Temple University Press, 1995), 172. On Adwo and other *abosom* linked to day of birth, see J. G. Christaller, *Dictionary of the Asante and Fante Language Called Tshi* (Basel: Basel Evangelical Missionary Society, 1933), 599.

12. Christian G.A. Oldendorp, *Historie der caribischen Inseln Sanct Thomas, Sanct Crux und Sanct Jan, insbesondere der dasigen Neger und der Mission der evangelischen Brüder unter denselben, part 1*, eds. Gudrun Meier, Stephan Palmié, Peter Stein, and Horst Ulbricht (Berlin: Staatliches Museum für Völkerkunde Dresden, 2000), 386.

13. Kofi Agyekum, professor of linguistics at the University of Ghana (Legon), recounts below (in English translation) the *adintoɔ* ceremony of his daughter held in June 1985 in Kumase. The form and text are strikingly similar to the general form outlined for Adwoa. Professor Agyekum's daughter, Afua Ataa Boakyewaa Agyekum, was named after his mother, a female twin born on Friday. The elder officiant of the *adintoɔ* ceremony said the following: "Baby, you are wel-

come to this world. Have a longer stay, just do not come and exhibit yourself and return. Your mothers and fathers have assembled here today to give you a name. The name we are giving to you is Afua Ataa Boakyewaa Agyekum. You are named Afua because that is the day your soul decided to enter into this world. We are naming you after your grandmother Afua Ataa. Your grandparent is Ataa because she was born a twin. Her real name is Boakyewaa, the feminine form of Boakye. Remember that your grandmother is a twin and, therefore, a deity and sacred figure that must be kept hallowed. In view of this, come and put up a good moral behavior. Again, we are attaching your father's name Agyekum to your name. Follow the footsteps of your father and come and study hard. When we say water let it be water, when we say drink let it be drink." Kofi Agyekum, "The Sociolinguistic of Akan Personal Names," *Nordic Journal of African Studies* 15, no. 2 (2006): 217.

14. In addition to interviews and conversations with knowledgeable Akan persons over the years, I have also consulted the following with regard to patrilineal lineages: Robert S. Rattray, *Ashanti* (Oxford: Clarendon Press, 1923), 47–49; Agyekum, "Sociolinguistic," 218; T. C. McCaskie, *State and Society in Pre-Colonial Asante* (New York: Cambridge University Press, 2003), 170–72; Gérard Pescheux, *Le royaume Asante (Ghana): Parenté, pouvoir, histoire, XVIIe–XXe siècles* (Paris: Karthala Editions, 2003), 293–98; A. Abu Boahen, E. Akyeampong, N. Lawler, T. C. McCaskie, and Ivor Wilks, eds., *"The History of Ashanti Kings and the Whole Country Itself" and Other Writing by Otumfuo Nana Agyeman Prempeh I* (New York: Oxford University Press, 2003); A. A. Opoku, *Obi Kyerɛ* (Tema: Ghana Publishing Co., 1973), 20–23, 26–30; B. S. Akuffo, *Tete Akorae* (Accra: Bureau of Ghana Languages, 1970), 71–74; E. R. Addow, *Edin ne Mmrane* (Accra: Bureau of Ghana Languages, 1969), 6; Thomas Yao Kani, *Akanfoɔ*

Amammerɛ (Accra: Bureau of Ghana Languages, 1962), 54–62; Kofi A. Busia, *The Position of the Chief in the Modern Political System of Ashanti* (New York: Oxford University Press, 1951); Christaller, *Dictionary*.

15. Algemeen Rijksarchief, The Hague, Collectie Leupe 743, dated December 25, 1629. This anonymous map is often attributed to Dutch cartographer Hans Propheet. The map had two sections: geographical features on the right, descriptive text on the left. The title on the map reads: "Map of the country of the Gold Coast in Guinea such that in various places [on this coast] I have questioned the most expert blacks and as far as our nation frequenting the coast has found compliant. It is collected for the first time for the use of those who include it in their speculation, until someone else updates it better. Done on December 25, anno 1629. In Guinea before Moure." For analysis, see K. Y. Daaku and A. van Dantzig, "Map of the Regions of Gold Coast in Guinea," *Ghana Notes and Queries* 9 (1966): 14–15; De Marees, *Description*, 77.

16. ANTT, TSO, IL, proc. 1604, f. 108r; *MMA*, 4, doc. 8; CC, parte 1, maço 4, no. 42; Duarte Pacheco Pereira, *Esmeraldo de Situ Orbis* (Lisbon: Imprensa Nacional, 1892), 69; Hair, Jones, and Law, *Barbot on Guinea*, 373, 381; De Marees, *Description*, 68, 72, 75–76, 78–82; Jones, *German Sources*, 86, 108, 153–54, 201–2, 256, 280.

17. *MMA*, 4, doc. 8; CC, parte 1, maço 4, no. 42; Pereira, *Esmeraldo*, 69; Hair, Jones, and Law, *Barbot on Guinea*, 373, 381; De Marees, *Description*, 68, 72, 75–76, 78–82; Jones, *German Sources*, 86, 108, 153–54, 201–2, 256, 280.

18. BNP, Fundo Geral, Mss. 8457, ff. 100v–101r. On the convicts and galleys in the Portuguese empire, see Timothy J. Coates, "The Portuguese Empire, 1100–1932," in *A Global History of Convicts and Penal Colonies*, ed. Clare Anderson (London: Bloomsbury Academic, 2018), 38–39, 45–46, 48. See also Timothy J. Coates, *Convicts and Orphans: Forced and*

State-Sponsored Colonizers in the Portuguese Empire, 1550–1755 (Stanford, CA: Stanford University Press, 2001); Timothy J. Coates, *Convict Labor in the Portuguese Empire, 1740–1932: Redefining the Empire with Forced Labor and New Imperialism* (Leiden: Brill, 2014).

19. ANTT, TSO, IL, proc. 1604, ff. 3–4v, 6v.
20. ANTT, TSO, IL, proc. 1604, ff. 15v, 17v, 23, 28v, 34, 37.
21. ANTT, TSO, IL, proc. 1604, ff. 101v, 103v, 109v. On communication, note that even the transiently present English in the mid-sixteenth century struggled to communicate, but recognized the need, pushing them to record a number of Akan words useful for trade while also using sign language— "made as signes to come againe the next day." The English voyagers confirm the early Portuguese records and the subsequent Dutch ones, in that the Akan/Twi language was the principal idiom on the coast and into the interior. Through phonetic English rendering, the earliest English specimens include such terms as *mate* ("mattea"), *daase* ("dassee"), *sika* ("sheke"), *ko twa* ("cowrte"), *fufuo* or *fugu* ("foco"). See Richard Hakluyt, *The Principal Navigations, Voyages, Traffiques and Discoveries of the English Nation* (London: J. MacLehose and Sons, 1906), 6: 206.
22. Martim Gonçalves was appointed vicar of Nossa Senhora da Conceição and administrator of the Ecclesiastical Jurisdiction of Mina by royal writs dated the 12th and the 15th of December 1571. See ANTT, *Chancelaria da Ordem de Cristo*, liv. 2, f. 43v. In the Chancery, we find a certain Jerónimo Dias, an ordained cleric, who was examined in letters and virtue by the Fathers of the Company of Jesus, and who was granted the office of chaplain of the church of Nossa Senhora da Conceição of Mina, on October 28, 1571. See ANTT, *Chancelaria da Ordem de Cristo*, liv. 2, f. 44. As there was a fear of backsliding and unconvinced converts, so too there was a distrust of New Christians (*Cristão-novo*) from Portugal, that is, those Jews and Muslims forcibly converted as a con-

dition of living in Portugal, after both groups were expelled from one part or another of Iberia (at slightly different times). A law issued years before, but without much enforcement, stipulated that no New Christians should come to Mina. The official requested this law be observed because, he reasoned, "They are greedier, more cunning, more mischievous, more shameless in defending their own interest, and more interested in others' property, than befits a reputable man" (cf. *MMA*, 2: 570).

23. ANTT, TSO, IL, proc. 1604, f. 101v; Jones, *German Sources*, 219, 244.

24. ANTT, TSO, IL, proc. 1604, ff. 101v, 102v; ANTT, Contos do Reino e Casa, Núcleo Antigo 867 (transcribed in J. Bato'ora Ballong-Wen-Mewuda, *São Jorge da Mina, 1482–1637: A vie d'un comptoir portugais en Afrique occidentale* (Lisbon: Fondation Calouste Gulbenkian, 1993), 2: 493–519); *MMA*, 1, doc. 61; CC, parte 1, maço 8, no. 116; De Marees, *Description*, 175–78. The Portuguese official had argued, "I do not agree with those who object that this [trade in melegueta] would lead to reducing the [trade in] spices from India, but rather know for certain that they are totally mistaken, for I believe that the amount of melegueta which is taken to those parts [of Europe] by robbers is the same as, or even greater than, what can be sent there [from India]." On melegueta peppers (grains of paradise), see Abena Dove Osseo-Asare, *Bitter Roots: The Search for Healing Plants in Africa* (Chicago: University of Chicago Press, 2014), 71–105.

25. ANTT, TSO, IL, proc. 1604, ff. 102r, 108r.

26. ANTT, TSO, IL, proc. 1604, ff. 108r–v, 109r.

27. ANTT, TSO, IL, proc. 1604, ff. 102r–v.

28. ANTT, TSO, IL, proc. 1604, f. 108; Contos do Reino e Casa, Núcleo Antigo 867; Pereira, *Esmeraldo*, 69.

29. ANTT, TSO, IL, proc. 1604, f. 105v; De Marees, *Description*, 110–14; Jones, *German Sources*, 85, 207 (emphasis added); Hakluyt, *Principal Navigations*, 6: 227 (emphasis added);

Rebecca Earle, "'If You Eat Their Food...': Diets and Bodies in Early Colonial Spanish America," *American Historical Review* 115, no. 3 (June 2010): 705.

30. ANTT, TSO, IL, proc. 1604, f. 105v. Samuel Brun, an early-seventeenth-century German-speaking observer, tells us, on the coast, "sheep is alien to them." See Jones, *German Sources*, 87.

31. ANTT, TSO, IL, proc. 1604, f. 104r.

32. ANTT, TSO, IL, proc. 1604, f. 104v.

33. ANTT, TSO, IL, proc. 1604, ff. 104v–105r; De Marees, *Description*, 173–74; Jones, *German Sources*, 122, 152.

34. ANTT, TSO, IL, proc. 1604, f. 106r.

35. ANTT, TSO, IL, proc. 1604, ff. 106v–107r.

36. ANTT, TSO, IL, proc. 1604, f. 107r.

37. ANTT, TSO, IL, proc. 1604, f. 107r.

38. John Vogt, *Portuguese Rule on the Gold Coast* (Athens: University of Georgia Press, 1978), 55–56, 122–23; *MMA*, 1: 426, 444, 502, 519; 2: 351, 513; 4: 87, 136; 8: 185; *MMA*, 3: 89–113; Ralph M. Wiltgen, *Gold Coast Mission History, 1471–1880* (Techny, IL: Divine Word Publications, 1956), 20; A. Teixeira da Mota and P. E. H. Hair, *East of Mina: Afro-European Relations on the Gold Coast in the 1550s and 1560s; An Essay with Supporting Documents* (Madison: University of Wisconsin, African Studies Program, 1988), 81, 93.

39. Ludewig Ferdinand Rømer, *Tilforladelig Efterretning om Kysten Guinea—A Reliable Account of the Coast of Guinea (1760)*, trans. and ed. Selena A. Winsnes (London: Oxford University Press for the British Academy, 2000), 162–63.

EPILOGUE

1. Adam Jones, ed., *German Sources for West African History, 1599–1669* (Wiesbaden: Franz Steiner Verlag, 1983), 176.

2. Jones, *German Sources*, 177–78. For the decline of Christian

affiliation in North America, see, for instance, Pew Research Center, "America's Changing Religious Landscape," May 12, 2015. By the nineteenth century, western Europe began losing its appetite for Christian dogma and church-going in favor of rational dogma as well as a brazen imperialism. Is it ironic these changes occurred when the greatest missionary activity was launched on impending colonial Africa and newly emancipated diasporic Africans in the Americas? Rejoicing in tales crafted by colonized and formerly enslaved converts as the principal source materials binds scholars and writers to the one-story problem, leaving us without the layered contexts of conversion and choice, of what was forever lost, and of the informed rejection of dogma and choosing otherwise.

3. Noel W. Solomons, "Diet and Long-Term Health: An African Diaspora Perspective," *Asia Pacific Journal of Clinical Nutrition* 12, no. 3 (2003): 313–30; Jeannette Y. Wick and Guido R. Zanni, "Diaspora, Disease, and Health Care," *Consultant Pharmacist* 22, no. 3 (2007): 223–28; Sarah A. Tishkoff and Scott M. Williams, "Genetic Analysis of African Populations: Human Evolution and Complex Disease," *Nature Reviews Genetics* 3 (2002): 617–18; James Nazroo et al., "The Black Diaspora and Health Inequalities in the US and England," *Sociology of Health and Illness* 29, no. 6 (2007): 811–30; Clarence Spigner, "Race, Health, and the African Diaspora," *International Quarterly of Community Health Education* 27, no. 2 (2006–7): 161–76; Sharon K. Okonkwo, "Consequences of the African Diaspora on Nutrition," *Nutrition Noteworthy* 5, no. 1 (2002), http://escholarship.org/uc/item/26n8m2j3, accessed December 1, 2020; Amy Luke et al., "Nutritional Consequences of the African Diaspora," *Annual Review of Nutrition* 21 (2001): 47–71.

4. James McCann, "Maize and Grace: History, Corn, and Africa's New Landscapes, 1500–1999," *Comparative Studies in Society and History* 43, no. 2 (2001): 260; James McCann, *Maize and Grace: Africa's Encounter with a New World Crop 1500–2000* (Cambridge, MA: Harvard University Press, 2005).

INDEX

INDEX

INDEX